Exchange rates and policy coordination

Exchange rates and policy coordination

Peter B. Kenen

University of Michigan Press
Ann Arbor

Published in the United States of America by
The University of Michigan Press

1992 1991 1990 1989   4 3 2 1

Library of Congress Cataloging in Publication Data applied for

ISBN 0-472-10141-2

Typeset in Great Britain
by Megaron, Cardiff

Printed in Great Britain
by Biddles Ltd., Guildford and King's Lynn

05/16/90

Contents

Preface

This book grows out of work begun in 1983–84 at the Australian National University, under a Professorial Fellowship awarded by the Reserve Bank of Australia. Some of the results appeared in *The Journal of Policy Modeling*, and an early version of the book appeared as a Brookings Discussion Paper in International Economics. I revised it extensively, however, when invited to give two lectures at the University of Manchester in February 1988.

Books acquire their own personalities long before they are finished. Revisions improve them but do not reform them. If I were starting this one again, I would try to give it a different personality. I would pay more attention to recent developments, most notably the changes in exchange-rate arrangements that have followed the Plaza and Louvre agreements. Instead, I have written another book, *Managing Exchange Rates*, to look at the future of the monetary system and the outlook for policy coordination. Each one borrows from the other, but they have different aims. This book seeks to synthesize arguments and evidence pertaining to the workings of the monetary system. That book seeks to show how it might be made to function more effectively.

Many colleagues have given me encouragement and criticism, including Michael Artis, Ralph Bryant, Richard Cooper, Max Corden, Gerald Holtham, Marcus Miller, Richard Portes, Jeffrey Sachs, and Robert Solomon, along with participants in seminars at the Australian National University, the International Monetary

Fund, Harvard University, Princeton University, the Royal Institute of International Affairs, and the University of Manchester.

I am grateful for generous financial support from the Reserve Bank of Australia, the Royal Institute of International Affairs, and the German Marshall Fund of the United States.

Chapter 1

Introduction

For most of its long history, international monetary theory has been concerned with the links between national monetary systems. It has asked how exchange-rate regimes influence the conduct and potency of national policies, how they condition the ways in which one country's policies affect other countries, and how those externalities can be internalized by multinational arrangements, rules of conduct for national governments, or looser arrangements broadly described as policy coordination.

There has been a striking change, however, in the subject as a whole and in discussions about policy coordination. The subject as a whole has been nationalized. Instead of stressing the links between national monetary systems under various exchange-rate regimes and thus ranking those regimes from a global or cosmopolitan standpoint, it has come to rank them from a single country's standpoint. It looks inward at the consequences for that country of the way that it chooses to link itself to the outside world, and the choice is treated as one that the country can make on its own, acting independently.[1]

Some of the literature strays even further from the traditional mode by dealing with optimal exchange-rate arrangements for a small economy, which is exposed to the effects of other countries' policies but does not affect them. What was once *The Economics of Interdependence* has become *Open Economy Macroeconomics*, and small-country macroeconomics at that.[2]

Academic and official discussions of policy coordination have also adopted a newly narrow framework. Those discussions are necessarily concerned with interactions between national policies and the internalization of those interactions. In much of the academic literature, however, the gains from policy coordination are measured from a national perspective:

> it is probably desirable to reserve for the term international policy *coordination* the more precise definition that is understood in the academic literature: the agreement by two or more countries to a cooperative set of policy changes, where neither would wish to undertake the policy change on its own but where each expects the package to leave it better off relative to the Nash noncooperative equilibrium in which each sets its policies taking the other's as given.[3]

This definition puts the problem of policy coordination into a familiar setting – the quest for Pareto optimality – which helps an economist to analyze it rigorously. In fact, it is used as the point of departure for the theoretical work presented in Chapter 3. Nevertheless, it is too narrow to explain how governments actually behave when they undertake to coordinate their policies.

With rather few exceptions, moreover, academic and official discussions of policy coordination have taken the exchange-rate regime as given. They tacitly accept existing arrangements, modified perhaps by more active management than was typical before the Plaza and Louvre agreements, as the only appropriate or feasible framework for international monetary cooperation.

This approach dodges a basic issue. The need to coordinate national policies arises from the size and character of the externalities produced by particular exchange-rate arrangements. When there is a shortage of policy coordination, two remedies can be considered. It may be possible to raise the supply of coordination by changing the governments' habits or to reduce the demand by changing exchange-rate arrangements. Attention has focused mainly on ways to raise the supply. Little has been said about reducing the demand, because it is still widely believed that floating exchange rates serve to minimize that demand.

Proposals for changing exchange-rate arrangements have been

made frequently in recent years, but not with the aim of reducing the demand for policy coordination. In fact, most of those proposals go in the opposite direction. They would call for more intensive coordination.

McKinnon has proposed a gradual return to fixed exchange rates, because he believes that floating rates destabilize the domestic demand for money and thus prevent individual governments from exploiting the autonomy that they were supposed to enjoy under floating rates.[4] Yet McKinnon's fixed-rate system would not give them more autonomy, even if it stabilized the demand for money. On the contrary, governments would be expected to accept a gold standard without gold that would put strict limits on national autonomy. The growth rate of the global money stock would be chosen jointly by the major governments, and each would adopt a growth rate for itself consistent with that global rate. It could depart from that national rate only when it had to defend its exchange rate by nonsterilized intervention in the foreign-exchange market.

Plans for using target zones to stabilize exchange rates are less doctrinaire about monetary management. Nevertheless, most advocates of target zones doubt that official intervention can play a major role in exchange-rate management. They would rely mainly on monetary policies to prevent exchange rates from wandering outside their zones.[5] Accordingly, the adoption of target zones could intensify rather than relieve the shortage of policy coordination. This is not to quarrel with the case for target zones, although there are reasons to wonder whether they can be an adequate framework for exchange-rate management.[6] It is merely to contrast the perspective adopted by the advocates of target zones, who would draw on the supply of policy coordination to stabilize exchange rates, with the perspective adopted later in this book, where exchange-rate regimes are judged by comparing the extent to which they reduce the demand for policy coordination.

Academic economists need not shoulder all the blame for the narrowly national focus of recent research and policy debate. Consider the language of the Second Amendment to the Articles of Agreement of the International Monetary Fund, which ratified the shift to floating exchange rates that took place five years earlier. Under Article IV, each member is required 'to collaborate with the Fund and other members to assure orderly exchange arrangements and to promote a stable system of exchange rates', but may choose its own arrangements. These include:

(i) the maintenance by a member of a value for its currency in terms of the special drawing right or another denominator, other than gold, selected by the member, or (ii) cooperative arrangements by which members maintain the value of their currencies in relation to the value of the currency or currencies of other members, or (iii) other exchange rate arrangements of a member's choice.

I once described this list as codified anarchy,[7] but others have defended it. The most cogent defense was offered by Corden, who sought to distil the 'logic' of the 'non-system' epitomized by Article IV:

The key feature of the present system is that it is a form of international *laissez-faire*. First of all, it allows free play to the private market, not just to trade in goods and non-financial services but, above all, to the private capital market. Secondly, it allows free play to governments and their central banks to operate in the market and – if they wish and where they can – to influence and even fix its prices or its quantities. Thus it is a fairly free market where many governments, acting in their own presumed interests and not necessarily taking much account of the interests of other governments, are participants.[8]

On this view, each government can and should be free to choose its own monetary and fiscal policies but also to choose its own exchange-rate arrangements and its stance as a net borrower or lender on the international capital market.[9]

This sort of decentralization might be optimal if all economies were small. One country's decisions regarding its exchange rate would barely affect other countries' effective exchange rates, and its decisions to borrow or lend would not greatly affect world interest rates. Large countries, however, do not have this atomistic independence. They cannot ignore the effects of their policies on other large countries, which can be expected to react and thus affect the outcome; nor can they be indifferent to the effects of their policies on the much larger number of small countries whose policy choices are constrained by the global economic environment produced by the large countries' policies.[10] Finally, Corden's *laissez-faire* approach ignores the fundamental proposition first articulated by Mundell. In a world of N independent countries there are only N-1 independent exchange rates. Therefore, it is arithmetically impossible for each country to choose its exchange-rate arrangements independently.[11]

This book has three objectives. First, I will attempt to show that policy coordination has been concerned in part with the pursuit of collective objectives, most notably the defense of international arrangements against economic and political shocks. Economic cooperation in general and policy coordination in particular have been regime-preserving enterprises rather than policy-optimizing exercises.[12] Therefore, policy coordination has been episodic and has rarely involved mutual modifications in domestic policies designed to take the participating countries from Nash to Pareto equilibrium. These assertions have extensive implications for the way in which economists should measure the gains from policy coordination, the frequency with which we can expect it to occur, and the roles of international institutions.

Second, I will assess the contributions made by recent academic work using the narrow but rigorous policy-optimizing framework. That work has illuminated many issues, even though it does not describe realistically the actual process of coordination. But it has cast some shadows too, by paying excessive attention to game-theoretic considerations. Governments engaged in policy coordination are treated as though they were oligopolists manoeuvering to dominate a market. This analogy tends to exaggerate the antagonistic aspects of the process and obscures two other aspects – the tendency of governments to disregard or underestimate the importance of foreign repercussions, including other governments' policy reactions, and their concern to defend international arrangements threatened by market or political forces. These two tendencies work in opposite directions, but both are influential within every government. Governments are not monolithic. Parts of every national bureaucracy are incorrigibly insular, but others are keenly aware of policy interdependence.

Finally, I will return to the basic question neglected in recent discussions – whether a shortage of policy coordination should be relieved by raising the supply or reducing the demand. More precisely, I will ask whether a change in exchange-rate arrangements could be helpful, given the political and institutional obstacles to continuous, finely tuned policy coordination. I will use the conventional policy-optimizing framework, but not for the usual purpose of measuring the gains from coordination. Instead, I will use it to measure the amounts of national autonomy that governments can be expected to enjoy under floating and pegged exchange rates– the extent to which they can achieve their national objectives by pursuing independent monetary policies rather than having to coordinate them closely. And I will come to an unusual conclusion. The economic interdependence produced by floating exchange rates may call for more coordination than the interdependence produced by fixed exchange rates. Accordingly, it may be better to return to a system of pegged but adjustable exchange rates than to strive for the close coordination required under floating rates.

Notes

1 Recent examples include Elhanan Helpman and Assaf Razin, 'A Comparison of Exchange Rate Regimes in the Presence of Imperfect Capital Markets', *International Economic Review*, 23 (June 1982), pp. 365–88, Don E. Roper and Stephen J. Turnovsky, 'Optimal Exchange Market Intervention in a Simple Stochastic Macro Model', *Canadian Journal of Economics*, 13 (May 1980), pp. 296–309, Jacob A. Frenkel and Joshua Aizenman, 'Aspects of the Optimal Management of Exchange Rates', *Journal of International Economics*, 13 (November 1982), pp. 231–56, Kent Kimbrough, 'The Information Content of the Exchange Rate and the Stability of Real Output under Alternative Exchange-Rate Regimes', *Journal of International Money and Finance*, 2 (April 1983), pp. 27–38, and Stephen J. Turnovsky, Exchange Market Intervention Policies in a Small Open Economy', in J. S. Bhandari and B. H. Putnam, eds., *Economic Interdependence and Flexible Exchange Rates* (MIT Press, 1984), pp. 286–311.

Small-economy models are not only inappropriate for comparing exchange-rate regimes but can be misleading in other ways. Currie and Levine compared simple rules for conducting monetary policies, including feedback rules based on the exchange rate, on nominal income, and on the price level, and contrasted them to fully optimal policies; working with a small open economy, they found that a simple price-level rule was quite robust for the five disturbances they examined, comparing favorably with optimal policies, but found that it was unsatisfactory when they turned to a two-country model. See David Currie and Paul Levine, 'Simple Macropolicy Rules for the Open Economy', *Economic Journal*, 95 (Supplement 1985), pp. 60–70.

2   I refer, of course, to Richard N. Cooper, *The Economics of Inter-dependence* (McGraw-Hill, 1968) and Rudiger Dornbusch, *Open Economy Macroeconomics* (Basic Books, 1980).

3   Jeffrey A. Frankel, *Obstacles to International Macroeconomic Policy Coordination*, Princeton Studies in International Finance, 64 (International Finance Section, Princeton University, 1988), p. 1.

4   Ronald I. McKinnon, *An International Standard for Monetary Stabilization*, Policy Analyses in International Economics, 8 (Institute for International Economics, 1984).

5   See, e.g, James E. Meade, 'A New Keynesian Bretton Woods', *Three Banks Review* (June 1984), pp. 8–25, and John Williamson, *The Exchange Rate System*, Policy Analyses in International Economics, 5, Revised Edition (Institute for International Economics, 1985). The most recent version of Williamson's proposal appears at times to contemplate a larger role for intervention, but it is not internally consistent on this issue; see John Williamson and Marcus H. Miller, *Targets and Indicators: A Blueprint for the International Coordination of Economic Policies*, Policy Analyses in International Economics, 22 (Institute for International Economics, 1987). For a survey of the literature on target zones, see Jacob A. Frenkel and Morris Goldstein, 'A Guide to Target Zones', *International Monetary Fund Staff Papers*, 33 (December 1986), pp. 633–73.

6   See Peter B. Kenen, *Managing Exchange Rates* (Royal Institute of International Affairs and Routledge, 1988), chs. 3–4.

7   Peter B. Kenen, 'Techniques to Control International Reserves', in R. A. Mundell and J. J. Polak, eds., *The New International Monetary System* (Columbia University Press, 1976), p. 208.

8   W. Max Corden, 'The Logic of the International Monetary Non-system', in F. Machlup, G. Fels, and H. Muller-Groeling, eds., *Reflections on a Troubled World Economy: Essays in Honor of Herbert Giersch* (St Martin's Press, 1982), p. 60.

9   A different defense of the 'market' approach is offered by Vaubel, who favors complete *laissez-faire*. Governments should compete in attempting to provide the most stable economic environment, measured primarily by price stability. Hence, policy coordination is harmful because it reduces competition among governments and may lead them to make the same errors

simultaneously rather than make mutually offsetting errors. See Roland Vaubel, 'Coordination or Competition among National Macroeconomic Policies?', in Machlup *et al.*, eds., *Reflections*, pp. 3–28.

10 Corden discusses these externalities in a subsequent paper, paying particular attention to fiscal policies. He concedes that large countries' budget deficits can have large effects on real exchange rates and world interest rates. But he does not depart substantially from his earlier 'market' view that each country should pursue its own fiscal policy, modified perhaps by some coordination. Countries can mitigate the adverse effects of their neighbors' policies by adjusting their own policies rather than relying on agreed rules or procedures to limit or correct fiscal-policy differences. See W. Max Corden, 'Fiscal Policies, Current Accounts and Real Exchange Rates: In Search for a Logic of International Policy Coordination', *Weltwirtschaftliches Archiv*, 122, no. 3, pp. 3–18.

11 Robert A. Mundell, 'Problems of the International Monetary System', in R. A. Mundell and A. K. Swoboda, eds., *Monetary Problems of the International Economy* (University of Chicago Press, 1969), p. 29. Ragnar Nurkse made the same point much earlier, when criticizing the decentralized setting of exchange rates after the First World War; see *International Currency Experience* (League of Nations, 1944), ch. v.

12 In an earlier paper, I described this sort of regime-preserving cooperation as Bergson-improving cooperation to distinguish it from Pareto-improving cooperation; see Peter B. Kenen, 'International Money and Macroeconomics', in K. A. Elliott and J. Williamson, eds., *World Economic Problems* (Institute for International Economics, 1988). That terminology is unsatisfactory, however, because the Bergsonian social welfare function does not necessarily include collective goals; it can be a simple sum of national welfare levels.

Chapter 2

Perspectives on policy coordination

Varieties of economic cooperation

Governments engage in many forms of economic cooperation, and many terms are used to describe them.[1] Three sorts of activity deserve particular attention.

Consultation

This term will be used to describe transactions involving an exchange of information without unilateral or collective commitments to utilize that information. Consultations can take place directly among governments, bilaterally and multilaterally, or with the intermediation of international institutions such as the International Monetary Fund (IMF) and the Organisation for Economic Cooperation and Development (OECD).

When international institutions are involved, consultations can occur bilaterally between the institution and a member government. This mode is illustrated by the regular consultations conducted under Article IV of the IMF's Articles of Agreement. Consultations can also occur among members of an institution with the assistance and advice of that institution. This mode is illustrated by the periodic meetings of the G-7 governments (Canada, France, Germany, Italy, Japan, the United Kingdom, and the United States) to engage in 'multilateral surveillance' of their national policies; the Managing Director of the IMF prepares a background paper and participates in the discussion. Finally, an international institution can compile information from its members in order to produce its own forecasts and analyses. This mode is illustrated by the processes involved in preparing the IMF's *World Economic Outlook* (WEO) and the OECD's *Economic Outlook*, which synthesize large amounts of information gathered from national governments.

The gains from gathering information are obvious enough, but the gains to governments from swapping information are not often emphasized, and the institutions that facilitate the process are not given enough credit. No government can know as much about other governments' forecasts and plans as it does about its own, and the gains from trade in information may be larger than the gains from other sorts of international cooperation.[2] And consultations go beyond the mere exchange of information. They involve interpretation and persuasion, as governments try to change their partners' policies.

These efforts at persuasion may be most effective when governments appeal to their partners' own objectives, rather than collective goals. In the words of an unnamed 'summiteer' quoted by Putnam and Bayne:

You don't go to the summit with the idea of 'making policy', or usually of reaching any great conclusions about world economic problems. Every nation goes there, first of all, to explain its own problems, and secondly, to see how far it can get others to help it with its own problems. I doubt if many of us go there saying 'Here is the central problem of world economic strategy. What measures should we all take to improve it?' We are all convinced of the value of an international trading system, so there is some attempt to take the world view, but basically we are most concerned about our own domestic problems.[3]

Yet Putnam and Bayne go on to note that 'summits at their most effective have represented precisely the recognition by national leaders that they cannot solve their own problems without attending to world problems',[4] and the steps that led to the Bonn summit of 1978, discussed below, focused on concerns about the 'world economy' as well as the participants' concerns about their own national economies.

On this broad definition, consultation occurs whenever officials get together. Students of summitry have frequently stressed the import- ance to national leaders of explaining the political and bureaucratic constraints they face at home and understanding those that face their partners, as well as the mutual understanding that has developed among the 'sherpas' who guide their leaders to the summit.[5] Participants in other international gatherings likewise stress the value of their informal contacts, especially in groups that meet regularly, such as the G-7 ministers and deputies and the central bankers' monthly sessions at the Bank for International Settlements (BIS). They are helpful not only because they inform the participants about their colleagues' problems but also because they bear on the questions of reputation and credibility that have attracted so much attention in the game-theoretic literature on policy coordination.

Coordination

This term will be used to denote instances in which governments make clearly defined, mutual commitments to alter their own policies in order to pursue a common objective or help each government to pursue its own objectives. Coordination involves a 'package' of policy changes that would not take place in its absence.[6]

The mutual commitments may relate to policy targets, as they did at the 1977 London summit, where they were expressed in terms of growth rates for real GNP, or to policy instruments, as they did at the 1978 Bonn summit, where they were expressed in terms of fiscal-policy changes. They may involve commensurate objectives, such as growth rates and inflation rates, or comparable instruments, such as tax-rate and interest-rate changes, but may also involve disparate objectives, as was the case at Bonn in 1978, where Germany and Japan agreed to change their fiscal policies and the United States agreed to change its energy policies.

It is important to distinguish clearly between commitments to take specific actions or achieve specific targets and mere promises to work for common goals or to combat common dangers. But this vital distinction does not necessarily coincide with the frequently drawn distinction between coordination and convergence. Convergence involves coordination when governments make operational commitments, whether expressed in terms of targets or instruments. But convergence is too often promised without any effort at quantification, and an outsider cannot know whether it involves coordination. It may therefore be wise to disinvent the term.[7]

Coordination can involve differently dated policy changes, including contingent commitments – promises to take specific actions if certain events occur in the future. These are the sorts of commitments implicit in policy rules. To qualify as instances of true coordination, however, such rules must involve firm, state-contingent promises to take clearly specified actions and should probably be framed with reference to readily measured events – numbers that come from the marketplace or some 'neutral' source and are not subject to manipulation, revision, or contentious interpretation. Furthermore, such rules must call for action, not merely for talk about action, which is perhaps a useful way to distinguish between true rules and mere indicators.[8]

Collaboration

This term will be used to denote situations in which governments take specific measures to achieve agreed objectives but do not make mutually binding commitments about their national policies.

Collaboration is best illustrated by instances involving bilateral or multilateral lending to help a government meet its obligations or pursue its own policy objectives. They frequently fall in the class of events described above as regime-preserving enterprises. In almost every instance, the borrower is expected to modify its policies or take on other obligations. Many examples come to mind: the stabilization loans of the 1920s, which helped Central European countries return to the gold standard; the US loan to Britain in 1946 and the Marshall Plan itself; the several support operations for sterling in the 1960s and 1970s; the joint operations of the 'gold pool' from 1961 to 1968; the 'rescue' of the dollar in November 1978; and the speedy provision of bridge loans to Mexico and Brazil at the start of the debt crisis in 1982 and 1983. On this definition, moreover, most forms of financial assistance from the IMF represent collaboration.

It is harder to classify promises by governments to intervene jointly on the foreign-exchange market. These are commitments to act collectively and have an agreed objective, but it is rarely possible for an outsider to know whether the participating governments are pledged to act together when exchange rates reach certain limits or merely to discuss the situation. (One wonders, indeed, whether the insiders know what they are pledged to do.) The commitments are explicit in the European Monetary System (EMS). The exchange-rate rule is stated in clear numerical form; it operates symmetrically; and it is supported by an unusual financial arrangement – the promise by each central bank to provide an unlimited amount of its currency when another central bank needs that currency for mandatory intervention. Furthermore, exchange-rate realignments are decided collectively, not unilaterally. The Bretton Woods System was less precise, because a member's access to the IMF was not automatic beyond the 'reserve tranche' and there was no clear-cut definition of 'fundamental disequilibrium' for a member to invoke when it had to justify an exchange-rate change. Most target-zone proposals are even less precise, and the ad hoc arrangements of the last few years, including the Louvre Accord 1987, have been even looser.[9]

A closer look at policy coordination

These definitions and illustrations suggest that international monetary history has been full of consultation and a good deal of collaboration but that there has been very little full-fledged coordination. They also support my earlier assertion that collaboration and coordination can best be described as regime-preserving enterprises. That was most certainly true of the support operations for sterling, the swap agreements and other arrangements erected to defend the dollar (including the General Arrangements to Borrow, set up to help the IMF assist the United States), and the London gold pool which functioned from 1961 to 1968. All of them were meant to combat speculation against the two key prices of the Bretton Woods System – the sterling-dollar exchange rate and the dollar price of gold.[10] It was likewise true of the energy measures taken at the 1978 and 1979 summit meetings, which sought to reduce the industrial countries' dependence on imported oil and thus reduce the ability of the

Organization of Petroleum Exporting Countries (OPEC) to raise oil prices. At the 1978 Bonn summit, the United States agreed to decontrol domestic oil prices; at the 1979 Tokyo summit, each participating country agreed to an oil-import target.[11]

Recent examples of regime-preserving cooperation include the bridge-loan financing for Mexico in 1982, which was meant to forestall an international banking crisis while Mexico was seeking longer-term financing from the IMF,[12] and the Plaza Communique of September 1985, which sought to engineer a depreciation of the dollar but was aimed fundamentally at containing protectionist pressures in the United States.[13]

Coordination during the Bretton Woods era

Many authors appear to believe that there was much more co-ordination under the Bretton Woods System than in recent years, because the United States was more responsive to the views and needs of other countries, and governments attached enormous importance to defending pegged exchange rates. In Kindleberger's words:

[The] commitment to consultative macroeconomic policies in annual summit meetings of seven heads of state has become a shadow play . . . with ceremony substituted for substance. The 1950's and 1960's, when serious discussions were held at the lowly level of Working Party No. 3 of the OECD, were superior because the United States and other countries took them seriously.[14]

Artis and Ostry take a similar view:

From the vantage point of today, it takes an effort to realize the extent to which parity changes were resisted at [that] time. Maintenance of a constant parity was treated as tantamount to maintenance of stable social arrangements, and the contemplation of parity changes as the equivalent of 'thinking the unthinkable'.[15]

But we should not exaggerate the extent of full-fledged coordination. Frank discussions took place regularly in Working Party 3 and other international bodies, and much pressure was brought to bear on countries whose domestic policies were seen to threaten the pegged-rate system:

within the ambit of WP-3 business, individual countries' balance-of-payments positions and policies were necessarily exposed to the analysis of other countries. In a system in which exchange rates are supposed to be fixed, . . . one must be able to see that there will be consistency between the forecasts and policies of individual countries. Because an exchange rate is two-sided, every country has a potential interest in ensuring that this consistency exists. The process of searching for consistency necessarily brings into sharp relief those facets of a country's policy posture which appear either unsustainable or undesirable from the viewpoint of other nations. It is important not to overstate the degree of cooperation, though. Exchange-rate decisions, among others, remained firmly the property of the individual country wishing to initiate a change; these were apparently not even discussed, let alone agreed, beforehand. Stronger forms of pressure than the confrontation of views nevertheless came to prevail when, after 1964, WP-3 was charged, at the suggestion of the G-10, with the duty to engage in 'multilateral surveillance'.[16]

There *was* a cooperative spirit in the 1960s, quite different from the spirit of the early 1980s, when major governments used international meetings, including the annual summit meetings, to win endorsements for their own domestic policies, believing that the world economy would take care of itself if each government would put its own house in order.[17] But the cooperation of the 1960s can best be described as close consultation supplemented by episodic collaboration.

The United States was criticized bluntly when other governments believed that it was not meeting its hegemonic obligation – the obligation to supply the all-important public good, steady growth without inflation – or was seen to be exporting instability to others. The United States, in turn, joined other governments in criticizing countries that ran large balance-of-payments deficits, which could undermine exchange-rate stability, and the industrial countries as a group came to the aid of deficit countries, directly and through the IMF, when those countries needed balance-of-payments financing to buy time for policy changes to take hold or to ward off speculative pressures. The followers engaged in collective nagging when they were dissatisfied with the leader, and the leader listened attentively; the leader then joined the followers in nudging any follower that strayed far from the pace set by the leader. Yet the record of the 1960s does not supply many instances that qualify fully as policy coordination, in which the major industrial countries agreed to a 'package' of policy changes.

The habits of the 1960s survive in modified form. Mutual criticism is combined with balance-of-payments financing in the EMS. Collective criticism of the United States has given way to more symmetrical mutual criticism involving the United States, Europe, and Japan, which must jointly produce the public good, economic stability. And they are criticized in turn by the developing countries, which consume that public good.

For instances of genuine coordination, however, we must go to the summits of 1977, 1978, and 1979. At the London summit in 1977, the participants adopted target rates of growth for real GNP, although they did not promise to make specific policy changes if they missed those targets. (As the targets were close to the governments' own forecasts, no actions were required to meet them if the forecasts were correct.) At the Tokyo summit in 1979, the participants agreed to limit their oil imports, although, once again, they did not promise to take specific actions to reach those goals. At the Bonn summit in 1978, the participants made the most ambitious agreement, committing themselves to specific policy changes to achieve their macroeconomic and energy objectives.

The Bonn summit of 1978

The Bonn summit has been analyzed thoroughly by others, and I will not rehearse its whole history here. But three aspects of that history deserve attention.

First, the Bonn agreement was the last step in a long process, played out publicly in the media and privately within the OECD and other institutions:

The Bonn summit of July 16–17, 1978 was merely the most memorable moment of a multifaceted process of international policy adjustment that required more than three years to unfold from its inception in 1976 until its consummation in 1979. Conceived in the first half of the decade as a response to the problems of Western recovery from the first oil shock, the suggestion for a coordinated program of global reflation, led by the 'locomotive' economies of the United States, Germany, and Japan received a powerful boost from the incoming Carter Administration. . . . On the other hand, the

Germans and the Japanese protested that prudent and successful economic managers should not be asked to bail out spendthrifts. This issue dominated Western economic diplomacy during 1977 and 1978.

At London in 1977 the summiteers could agree only to play for time on the key questions. Although the Germans and Japanese accepted ambitious growth targets, they avoided commitments to fiscal expansion. . . . All sides conceded that the world economy was in serious trouble, but it was not clear which was more to blame – tight-fisted German and Japanese fiscal policies, or slack-jawed US energy and monetary policies.

Throughout the spring of 1978, negotiations that sprawled across a half-dozen bilateral and multilateral forums produced the outline of a possible package deal for the forthcoming Bonn summit. The heart of the bargain would be German agreement to specific reflationary measures, in return for specific American commitments on energy, especially the control of oil prices. Other elements in the proposed accord were Japanese export restraint and confirmation of an earlier commitment to domestic growth; American recognition of the risks of inflation; and acquiescence by the other countries (particularly the reluctant French) to a successful conclusion of the Multilateral Trade Negotiations. At the summit itself in Bonn in July, after some dickering about the details, this package was approved, the clearest case of a summit deal that left all participants happier than when they arrived.[18]

The outcome has been criticized vigorously, especially in Germany, where it is blamed for the emergence of large budget deficits and the resurgence of inflation – a view that disregards the role of the second oil shock. But there is wide agreement on the uniqueness of the process that led to the Bonn agreement and on the completeness with which it was implemented.[19]

Second, the process that led to the Bonn summit was concerned with collective objectives, as well as the domestic aims of the participating countries. This theme runs through the following passage, which is useful also in describing the role played by the OECD, not only as a forum but also as a catalyst:

The job of following up on the London summit had been given to the OECD, and at the June 1977 ministers' meeting the governments agreed to submit to the secretariat in October their national current account and growth projections for 1978. After compiling these forecasts in the fall, the secretariat calculated that the governments expected a collective growth rate for the OECD area as a whole of 4.5 per cent in 1978. The secretariat believed, however, that this was unrealistically high, given the national policies in place at the time, and that the area growth rate would not exceed 3.5 per cent, the outcome for 1977, without further stimulative measures. However, the secretariat recommended a 'differentiation' between policies of individual countries in the area, permitting each to focus on different objectives which would collectively raise growth and improve the pattern of current account payments.

The secretariat presented this argument at the November 1977 EPC meeting . . . and was given the go-ahead to develop a proposal for a joint reflation program in detail at the February 1978 EPC meeting. On the basis of this mandate, the secretariat asked each member government (a) the extent to which they could take expansionary measures, (b) what specific measures these might be, and (c) what would be the effects on them of other countries taking hypothetical expansionary or anti-inflationary measures. The secretariat, working sometimes very closely with US officials, then constructed a program of what it argued would be mutually consistent policy actions. This program was presented to member countries at the EPC meeting in May 1978 . . . [and] was broadly endorsed at the ministers' meeting shortly thereafter, though the specific policy contributions of each country were not made public in the meeting's communique. The countries on whom the program essentially depended remained noncommittal until the heads of government met at the economic summit in Bonn in July.[20]

It would be foolish to pretend that governments leave their domestic objectives behind when they go to international meetings to bargain about policies. It would be equally wrong, however, to interpret the bargaining process entirely in terms of narrowly defined national objectives. It may be more useful to view those objectives as boundaries on the governments' willingness to bargain, 'incentive-compatibility constraints' in the current jargon, and that is how they functioned before and during the Bonn summit.

Third, the Bonn agreement was not concerned exclusively with macroeconomic policies. President Carter made representations about US aims and plans, but they were rather vaguely worded:

He declared that reducing inflation was his top economic priority, and pointed to the reduction in the size of the 1979 tax cut, the voluntary wage and price programs and efforts to eliminate inflationary government regulations as evidence of his seriousness. . . . Nor were the American commitments in the macroeconomic field so specifically negotiated as the German commitment had been. The anti-inflation commitment was of secondary importance; the oil-price concession was the decisive *quid pro quo* to the German stimulus.... Nor did the American President promise anything new in the way of US commitments to support the dollar on the exchange markets.[21]

The scenario produced by the OECD, described in an earlier quotation, dealt exclusively with macroeconomic policies. That was the only sort of scenario it could produce, given its mandate. It might have been possible, moreover, to strike a simple single-issue bargain at the summit itself – to exchange an operational American commitment to combat inflation by tighter monetary and fiscal policies for German and Japanese commitments to raise their growth rates by easier fiscal policies. But the actual agreement was a cross-issue bargain, because the decontrol of oil prices was seen by all to be the most valuable commitment that the United States could make.

Artis and Ostry criticize cross-issue bargaining, even though they describe as 'exemplary' the process that produced the Bonn agreement: 'Although extending the area of coordination extends the range of potential policy improvement by increasing the possibility of policy bargains, negotiation and computation costs rise very rapidly with an increase in the spread of issues under negotiation.'[22] But Putnam and Henning disagree, even though they concede that the Bonn summit might have struck a simple single-issue bargain:

It can be shown formally – and Bonn demonstrates practically–that without cross-issue linkage, many important positive-sum international games may never be concluded. Thus, the potential gains from international economic policy coordination may be much greater in a multi-issue context than when coordination is confined to 'policy barter' within a single domain.[23]

The menu of issues cannot be too long without raising the difficult problem stressed by Artis and Ostry, but it cannot be too short without risking a breakdown in bargaining because the parties cannot agree on a balanced package lying wholly in a single policy domain. And a balanced package is absolutely necessary for governments to reach agreement on matters that are tangled up with domestic politics, such as fiscal policies. No government wants to be seen as giving without getting, and each one would like to claim that it got more than it gave. Furthermore, 'Each national leader already has made a substantial investment in building a particular coalition at the domestic [game] board, and he or she will be loath to construct a different coalition simply to sustain an alternative policy mix that might be more acceptable internationally.'[24] The high costs of building a new coalition or consensus must be worthwhile, which means that each leader must truly believe that he is getting more than he is giving.

These observations have another implication. Major changes in domestic policies cannot be negotiated by bureaucracies. Summitry is needed. On the one hand, national bureaucracies are too compartmentalized to weigh the economic and political costs and benefits of cross-issue bargaining. That is the politicians' task.[25] On the other hand, national and international bureaucracies 'are unlikely to break from inertial decision-making and established government policy positions in the absence of clear directives from the most senior political level'.[26] Much is wrong with summitry, but it has a vital part to play in policy coordination. It will come up again in the next chapter.

Limitations of the policy-optimizing framework

Economists have done much new research on policy coordination in the last few years, using and extending the game-theoretic approach adopted by Hamada a decade ago.[27] They have dealt with four important questions: (1) How large are the potential gains from policy coordination? (2) How can coordination be sustained when governments are tempted to renege on their promises? (3) What happens when governments are guided by conflicting views about economic structure and behavior? (4) Can reliance on policy rules, including exchange-rate rules, substitute for fully optimal policy coordination?

Interesting answers have been given, but they have been strongly influenced by some special suppositions about behavior by governments and markets.

Three restrictive assumptions

First, policy coordination is usually treated as an antagonistic process. Governments are deemed to bargain about the settings of their policy instruments, the growth rates of their money stocks, for instance, while concealing their views about the future, about basic economic processes, and about the benefits and costs of the particular policy changes under consideration. This leaves little or no scope for mutual persuasion – an appeal to the interests of the other participants, let alone to common or systemic concerns. Furthermore, it probably ascribes far too much influenced to the interactive aspects of policy formation – the governments' ability and willingness to swap specific policy changes and the attention that they give to other countries' policies when choosing their own policies unilaterally.

In the typical representation of policy coordination, each government's behavior is described by a reaction curve, showing how it will adjust its own policy instruments in response to a change in another country's instrument. All other exogenous variables affecting its policies are treated as determining the position of the curve. It would be more realistic to describe each government as setting its own policies with reference to its forecasts of the gaps between prospective and desired values of its target variables – the terms that appear in the typical welfare function – and thus treating other countries' policies as a subset of the many exogenous variables affecting its forecasts.

The two representations do not differ formally when governments are fully informed and can forecast accurately all of the variables affecting their economies, including other countries' policies. It is then possible to treat a government's forecasts of the gaps between prospective and desired values as functions of its forecasts of other countries' policies, along with all other exogenous variables, and the settings of its policy instruments can be deemed to depend on those forecasts. That is how reaction curves are derived. The difference in representations is very important, however, when governments do not forecast other countries' policies or fail to give them appropriate weight, but lump them with the other exogenous variables whose values they hold constant because they cannot forecast them.[28]

Second, governments are assumed to plan and announce future policies or to follow policy rules that have clear-cut implications for their future policies, and the private sector is assumed to have rational expectations, so that it can forecast correctly the effects of those future policies. This is the context in which economists typically analyze the problem of reneging, because forward-looking policy plans may be time inconsistent. As a government travels along its policy path, it will reach a point at which switching to a new path will be advantageous, although the switch will violate the government's promises to its own citizens or to other governments. The time inconsistency of optimal policies offers a neat way to pose the problem of reneging, but it is no more than that – an illustration – and may not be the most important aspect of the problem.

Third, much of the recent literature dwells on the limiting case of perfect capital mobility. Asset holders are deemed to be risk neutral, so that securities denominated in different currencies become perfect substitutes. In this limiting case, however, sterilized intervention in the foreign-exchange market – intervention that does not affect the money supply – cannot affect the exchange rate. Therefore, a government must choose between using its monetary policy to pursue its domestic policy objectives and allowing its exchange rate to float, or using its monetary policy to peg the exchange rate. It cannot do both. In consequence, the pegging of exchange rates is typically viewed as a second-best alternative to the optimal coordination of monetary policies aimed at achieving national or global objectives. Governments cannot peg exchange rates and also coordinate their monetary policies, except in a very limited sense.[29]

Clearly, this framework cannot be used to study the effects of various exchange-rate regimes on the process of coordination, the gains from coordination, or what was described above as the demand for coordination. These matters can be studied only by assuming that asset holders are risk averse rather than risk neutral, so that securities denominated in different currencies are imperfect substitutes and sterilized intervention is effective. That is the framework adopted in the next chapter, which examines the demand for coordination under floating and pegged exchange rates.

What do we know about the effectiveness of sterilized intervention? Many economists have tried to test the validity of the underlying behavioral assumptions by asking if the foreign-exchange market is efficient in the finance-theoretic sense. If asset holders were risk neutral and could forecast the exchange rate rationally, the forward rate would be an unbiased predictor of the future spot rate. It is not.[30] But this test is not decisive. It may merely say that expectations are not rational or that rationality cannot be represented by using the realized spot rate to stand for the expected rate, because of the so-called peso problem or the presence of rational bubbles.[31] Other economists have used econometric models to simulate the effects of sterilized intervention and shown them to be smaller and less durable than the effects of nonsterilized intervention.[32] Rogoff has found that sterilized intervention does not affect the exchange rate significantly, but Loopesco, Lewis, and others have found that it does.[33] The debate is far from over, making it prudent to be rather skeptical about conclusions drawn from models that rely crucially on the effectiveness of sterilized intervention, as well as those drawn from models based on perfect capital mobility.

The gains from policy coordination

Oudiz and Sachs were the first to quantify the gains from policy coordination.[34] They compared noncooperative and cooperative policies for the United States, Germany, and Japan, using large econometric models to run three sets of simulations. One simulation dealt with the actual state of the world; the second dealt with the effects of another oil shock; and the third dealt with the effects of altering US policies to produce a large reduction in the US current-account deficit. In each instance, Oudiz and Sachs asked how policy coordination would alter the settings of the three countries' policy instruments, how close they would get to their various policy targets, and how much welfare they would gain given their own welfare functions. Their simulations covered a three-year period (1984–86) and used two global models, the Federal Reserve Multicountry Model (MCM) and the Japanese Economic Planning Agency (EPA) model.

In this and every other effort to measure the gains from co-ordination, a difficult question crops up right away: What are the countries' welfare functions? Oudiz and Sachs give an ingenious but controversial answer. They treat their baseline simulation, reflecting the three countries' actual policies, as the Nash equilibrium, assign arbitrary targets to each of the three governments, then make their model reveal the weights that each government would have to give its targets in order to be in that Nash equilibrium. (The three governments were assumed to desire complete elimination of the GNP gap and zero inflation; the United States was assumed to desire current-account balance, but Germany and Japan were assumed to desire current-account surpluses equal to two per cent of GNP.)

Table 1 reproduces the welfare weights they obtained from the MCM model, and the results of their first simulation, concerned with

Table 1 *A summary of the Oudiz-Sachs results*

Statistic	United States	Germany	Japan
Welfare weights:			
Output	0.07	0.03	0.06
Inflation	0.37	0.37	0.52
Current account	0.00	0.68	4.35
Output gap:			
Noncooperative	5.44	10.70	6.01
Cooperative	4.46	9.74	4.76
Inflation rate:			
Noncooperative	4.38	2.99	2.65
Cooperative	4.54	3.23	2.69
Policy changes:			
Monetary policy	− 2.14	− 5.80	− 5.50
Fiscal policy	0.52	− 0.21	− 1.15
Welfare gain	0.17	0.33	0.99

Source: Gilles Oudiz and Jeffrey Sachs, 'Macroeconomic Policy Co-ordination Among the Industrial Countries', *Brookings Papers on Economic Activity*, 1, 1984, Tables 11 and 12.

improving the actual (baseline) outcome. The output gaps and inflation rates are annual averages for 1984–86; the changes in monetary policies are once-for-all percentage-point changes in discount rates made at the start of the simulation; the changes in fiscal policies are once-for-all changes in government spending expressed as percentage points of GNP; and the welfare gains are expressed in units equivalent to percentage-point changes in GNP averaged over 1984–86. In this particular simulation, coordination called for monetary and fiscal expansion by the United States and a mix of monetary expansion and fiscal contraction by Germany and Japan, but the fiscal-policy changes are small, and so are the effects on the output gaps and on the inflation rates. Therefore, the welfare gains are small (though larger than the gains obtained from the EPA model).[35]

Reviewing the results of these and other computations, Oudiz and Sachs conclude that:

Those who advocate a coordinated expansion as the solution to global unemployment must be presuming (a) a much larger group of countries taking policy actions in response to coordination, (b) a much higher degree of macroeconomic interdependence than appears in the EPA model and the MCM, or (c) objective functions that differ significantly from those of current policy makers. To put the last point another way, it appears to be the anti-inflation bias (or anti-Keynesian views) of policymakers rather than the absence of effective coordination that blocks a general reflation.[36]

The second and third possibilities, using models in which spillover effects are larger and using other welfare functions, have been studied extensively. Much of this research, however, has tended to confirm the Oudiz-Sachs conclusion that the gains from policy coordination are rather small when defined and measured in terms of the governments' own welfare functions.

Several objections have been raised against the way that Oudiz and Sachs extracted welfare weights from their baseline simulation, by assuming that it represents the Nash equilibrium. First and most obviously, the initial situation may not represent any sort of equilibrium. Economists have invested hugely in the notion of equilibrium and hesitate to raise this possibility, but political scientists can contemplate it fearlessly. Thus, Putnam and Henning suggest that the apparent US indifference to current-account deficits 'probably reflects an impasse in the domestic political game about the budget deficit, rather than a considered national choice'.[37] And a senior official made the same point in an off-the-record talk to an academic conference on policy coordination. 'We don't optimize', he said. 'We muddle'. But cogent objections have been raised even by those who are more sympathetic to the Oudiz-Sachs approach.

Many economists have noted that the need for policy coordination arises when each government has too few policy instruments to pursue its targets effectively. When it has as many instruments as targets, a government can go it alone, and there will be no gains from coordination.[38] In the Oudiz-Sachs exercise, each government has two instruments, fiscal and monetary policies, and the United States has two targets, because it assigns zero weight to its current-account balance. Therefore, the United States cannot be expected to gain from policy coordination and should not participate in it.[39]

Finally, the Oudiz-Sachs approach cannot be expected to produce valid welfare weights unless they are extracted from the same sort of model that governments use to choose their policies. The Oudiz-Sachs weights for Germany and Japan say that those countries are chiefly concerned with fighting inflation and defending their current-account surpluses, not combatting unemployment. But Marris suggests that these weights really reflect the two governments' views about economic behavior, not their true policy preferences:

If told that this was their motivation, German and Japanese policymakers would immediately respond that they have a quite different view of the 'truth' about how fiscal policy works. Most explicitly for the Germans, they believe that fiscal restraint, while depressing output in the short run, will – because of improved confidence and 'crowding in' – lead to higher output two or three years hence. If one substituted models with these properties, one would radically change not only the magnitude but also the sign of most of the results given in [the Oudiz-Sachs] paper.[40]

Elsewhere, Marris suggests that the Oudiz-Sachs weights may be more valid for some years than others:

after the second oil crisis economic cooperation actually itself introduced a deflationary bias into the system. What happened was that the major powers became convinced – in my view rightly – that they had to do something decisive about inflation. So whenever they met together they tried to bolster each other's courage to do it. It was not that they were Prisoner Dilemmaed, they were deliberately and collectively summoning up the courage to put us through the worst post-war recession – and most (but not all) of them knew what they were doing. So if we want to analyze this period with our nice new tools one should introduce a shift variable for this change in the major powers' preference function – which they then effectively imposed on the rest of the world.[41]

The danger resides in combining these revealed preferences with models far more Keynesian than the governments' own views.

Nevertheless, two more papers use the Oudiz-Sachs approach to see if there may be other reasons for the rather small welfare gains from policy coordination. Oudiz examines policy coordination within the European Community where, he suggests, high unemployment rates may reflect the governments' failure to coordinate their policies rather than the least-cost consequence of coordinated efforts to combat inflation, and the gains from policy coordination should be rather large because of big spillover effects.[42] Here again, however, the policy effects and welfare gains are rather small, because governments attach more weight to fighting inflation than reducing unemployment. Canzoneri and Minford examine the gains from transatlantic coordination using the Liverpool model, where the spillover effects of monetary policies are very large.[43] The gains from coordination are bigger than those reported by previous studies, but their size was found to depend not only on the size of the spillover effects but also on the character and size of the initial shock or disequilibrium that challenged the governments to act.[44]

A number of studies have used hypothetical welfare functions to measure the gains from policy coordination. A paper by Hughes Hallett[45] is especially interesting because it contains a revealing two-stage comparison. When welfare weights are chosen arbitrarily, the baseline simulation will not normally represent a Nash equilibrium, and two simulations are needed – one to measure welfare in the Nash equilibrium and another to measure the welfare gains from policy coordination. Hughes Hallett shows both calculations, using a modified version of the COMET model and dealing with policy coordination between the United States and Europe. Here are his welfare measures:[46]

Simulation	United States	European Community
Baseline	466.2	346.2
Noncooperative	103.6	81.3
Cooperative	96.2	55.8

These are loss-function calculations, so reductions are good things, but those that take place at the first stage, on the way from the baseline or 'muddle' to optimal noncooperative policies, are much larger than those that take place at the second, on the way from that Nash equilibrium to optimal policy coordination.

Finally, Holtham and Hughes Hallett[47] have used several multi-country models to compute and compare the gains from policy coordination and have worked with welfare functions that contain an unusually large number of targets – growth rates of real GNP, inflation rates, exchange rates, trade balances, levels of government spending relative to GNP, and growth rates of money stocks. (The last two are instruments, not targets, but figure in the welfare functions partly because of the costs of altering those instruments. Exchange rates are included to allow for the various costs of changes in nominal and real rates.) The gains from policy coordination vary from model to model, but tend to be larger than those reported in most other papers, and that is still true when exchange rates are dropped from the welfare functions. Holtham and Hughes Hallett present results for seven models and for two 'consensus' models, one based on four models which do not impose model-consistent (rational) expectations (NRE), and another based on the three models which do impose those expectations (RE). Here are the gains from policy coordination expressed as percentage reductions in the national loss functions and in units equivalent to average annual percentage gains in real GNP:[48]

Model	United States	Rest of OECD
Reduction in loss function:		
NRE consensus model	76.2	77.1
RE consensus model	90.1	82.1
Increase in real GNP:		
NRE consensus model	3.3	4.9
RE consensus model	6.7	6.8

These numbers are much bigger than those reported by most other studies, including studies based on the same models that Holtham and Hughes Hallett used.[49]

Reneging and sustainability
The problem of reneging or cheating and its implications for the sustainability of policy coordination have attracted more attention from economists than any other problem commonly cited as an obstacle to coordination – disagreement about policy objectives, forecasts, and the functioning of the world economy, or the interference of domestic political constraints. The problem is typically posed by building a model in which the government has an incentive to cheat because of the time inconsistencies in optimal policy plans. These arise, in turn, from the inability of the private sector to revise or modify its behavior without delay or cost.

The standard approach to the problem is easily illustrated by a simplified version of the case considered by Rogoff and others.[50] Wages and prices are set by the private sector in light of its expectations concerning the inflation rate, which depend on its expectations concerning the money supply. Suppose that the government promises to raise the money supply at a particular rate and that the private sector expects the government to keep its word. Wages and prices will be set accordingly, determining the actual inflation rate. At this point, the government has two options. If it keeps its promise, it will exactly validate the actual inflation rate, and there will be no change in output or employment. If it breaks its promise and raises the money supply faster, it will stimulate output and employment, because the actual inflation rate cannot change immediately. In other words, the government can exploit the time inconsistency produced by the short-run rigidity of the money wage.

If the government breaks its word frequently, however, it will lose credibility. The private sector will cease to pay attention to the government's promises; it will start to base its expectations on the rapid growth of the money supply that the government has been delivering rather than the low rate that it has been promising. The inflation rate will rise, and the rapid growth of the money supply will serve merely to validate the higher inflation rate. It can no longer stimulate output and employment.[51]

Rogoff has used this framework to show that international policy coordination can be welfare-reducing because it can raise the inflation rate over the long run.[52] In an open economy with a floating exchange rate, the government will have less scope to exploit short-run wage rigidity than it has in a closed economy or in an open economy with a pegged exchange rate. If it raises the growth rate of the money supply to stimulate employment, the domestic currency will depreciate, raising the price level by more than it would rise in a closed economy having the same wage rate initially. Hence, the government will keep the money supply from growing as rapidly, and the long-run path of the open economy will display a lower inflation rate. When governments coordinate their policies, however, and act jointly to exploit short-run wage rigidity, they can prevent exchange rates from changing. Therefore, their money supplies will grow faster than they would without coordination and will raise the long-run inflation rate – the one that will come to prevail eventually when each country's private sector bases its wage bargaining on the actual behavior of the money supply rather than the governments' promises.

There is a much larger point at issue here, however, pertaining to the sustainability of policy coordination. If governments bargain about future policy paths and the optimal paths are time inconsistent, governments will be tempted to cheat on each other, as well as to cheat on the private sector. It may therefore be hard for them to make any bargain initially, because they do not trust each other, let alone to make new bargains after they have broken old ones. To be sure, governments value their reputations. Furthermore, those that are most likely to cooperate in macroeconomic matters have also to cooperate in other economic and political domains. They will not lightly jeopardize their ability to do so by breaking their bargains deliberately. They stand to lose more by damaging their reputations than they can hope to gain by exploiting time inconsistencies in their macroeconomic plans.[53]

Yet many economists discount these considerations, because they believe that politicians are short-sighted. Therefore, they recommend that governments constrain themselves to time-consistent policies, even when those policies are not fully optimal when viewed in isolation, without regard to their reputational effects or the gains from international cooperation in other policy domains. Instead of trying to foreswear in advance the exploitation of future opportunities to cheat, governments are told to protect themselves and their successors from the temptation to cheat by rejecting time-inconsistent policies. That is the recommendation made by Miller and Salmon and by Oudiz and Sachs and adopted by McKibbin and Sachs in their simulations.[54] It is unattractive, however, because the gains from policy coordination can be small or negative when governments constrain themselves to time-consistent policies.[55]

Fortunately, this whole debate may miss the point completely. On the one hand, the gains from exploiting time inconsistencies may be rather small compared to the gains from using newly available information or adjusting policy plans to deal with new disturbances. On the other hand, the inability of governments to bind themselves and their successors may be quite important but for reasons different from those economists have emphasized.

Recent research on the choice of policy paths assumes that the government faces some initial disturbance or disequilibrium and chooses a policy path that takes its economy to long-run equilibrium. The world does not work that way. 'Disturbances . . . do not queue up, like aircraft in a holding pattern, waiting for the ones that went before to get out of the way.'[56] They bombard economies in quick succession, and policies have to be adjusted frequently. The policy path cannot be charted immutably. It must be conditioned explicitly or implicitly on the current state of the world and on current forecasts about the future. If those forecasts are confounded, policies must change. Therefore, policy changes do not necessarily call into question a government's credibility or damage its reputation, except in the theorist's world where every inhabitant of the economy knows enough to identify each new disturbance immediately and thus decide whether the government is reneging on its current policy plan or revising that plan appropriately to deal with a new situation.[57] Furthermore, a doggedly determined effort to follow a rigid policy plan despite a change in circumstances will undermine a government's reputation for good sense more quickly and decisively than a change in policy will undermine its reputation for good faith.

The alleged inconstancy of democratic governments is likewise exaggerated. It is obviously true that governments cannot bind their successors, and this is consequential, but not for the reason usually given. A government that faces an election soon and has any hope of winning will want to conserve its reputation at home and abroad. It will be reluctant to break explicit or implicit bargains. (It may even reduce its chances of winning the election by promising to make major policy changes rather than running on its record.) A newly elected government, moreover, has to establish its own reputation for reliability and is apt to honor inherited commitments unless they are wholly inconsistent with its basic aims.

Which brings us to the main point about a new government. It may decide to violate inherited commitments, not to exploit time inconsistencies in its predecessor's plans but because it has come into office with new objectives – a different welfare function. Politicians sometimes win elections by promising to be more effective than their rivals; more often, they promise new and different policies. Unfortunately, this important possibility does not have intriguing analytical properties and attracts much less attention than the comparatively minor problem of time inconsistency.[58]

How do governments handle these problems? First, they make treaties, which bind states, not merely governments, and are thus likely to be honored. This sort of solution is proposed by economists who favor the writing of a new constitution for the international monetary system – one that would promulgate transparently simple policy rules as second-best substitutes for optimal policy coordination. Second, governments try to avoid making commitments they cannot expect to honor and to honor those they make. This is the aspect emphasized by political scientists:

If we take seriously the claim that policy-makers in an anarchic world are constantly tempted to cheat, certain features of the [1978] Bonn story – certain things that did *not* happen – seem quite anomalous. We find little evidence that the negotiations were hampered by mutual fear of reneging. For example, even though the Bonn agreement was negotiated with exquisite care, it contained no special provisions about phasing or partial conditionality that might have protected the parties from unexpected defection. Moreover, the Germans and the Japanese both irretrievably enacted their parts of the bargain in September, more than six months before the President's action on oil price decontrol and nearly two years before decontrol was implemented.

Once the Germans and Japanese had fulfilled their parts of the bargain, the temptation to the President to renege should have been overpowering, if the standard account of international anarchy is to be believed. Moreover, the domestic political pressure on him to renege was clearly very strong. But virtually no one on either side of the final decontrol debate dismissed the Bonn pledge as irrelevant.[59]

All of which is not so very surprising when we take a broad view of policy coordination, stressing the role of persuasion, the pursuit of collective objectives as well as narrower national objectives, and the continuing, close, and complex relationships among the participating governments. At Bonn, each government stood to gain from its own 'concessions' as well as those extracted from its partners, and each was concerned to preserve its reputation for reliability. In President Carter's words, 'Each of us has been careful not to promise more than he can deliver.'[60]

Disagreements about economic behavior
Rogoff has shown that policy coordination can be welfare-worsening when the private sector is very well informed.[61] Frankel and Rockett have shown that it can be welfare-worsening when governments are

badly misinformed – when they do not understand how their economies operate.[62]

Frankel and Rockett use ten large multicountry models to represent US and European views about the world economy and assume that each government uses its model to measure the welfare effects of striking a bargain with the other. Each government holds its own views with certainty and knows those of the other too. But they do not try to influence the other's views. Instead, they strike a bargain whenever each government's calculations lead it to believe that it will gain, given its own views about the world, and they find that each government will expect to benefit whenever its views are correct, regardless of the other's views.

By way of example, these are the gains that the US government will expect to reap from policy coordination, measured in terms of its own welfare function, when its views about the world economy are represented by the Federal Reserve's Multicountry Model (MCM) and it is an accurate representation, but the composite European government holds views represented by the MCM, the Sims-Litterman Vector Autoregression Model (VAR), the OECD's Inter-link Model (OECD), and the Project Link Model (LINK), and the gains that the European government will expect to reap when its views are represented by the MCM but various views are ascribed to the US government:[63]

| Model ascribed | Welfare gain expected by | |
to partner	US	Europe
MCM	0.0002	0.0001
VAR	0.0001	0.0001
OECD	0.0001	0.0333
LINK	0.0001	0.0003

These gains are very small, but there are no losses. Therefore, both governments should be willing to coordinate their policies when they are deemed to bargain about their policy instruments, without exchanging information about their models, forecasts, or policy objectives or sharing analyses concerning the effects of the policy changes they propose.

What happens, however, when governments are wrong about the workings of the world economy? After they have taken the two governments through the bargaining process and know the new settings of the policy instruments, Frankel and Rockett ask what will happen to the world economy using the 'true' model. As they work with ten different models, they must analyze 100 policy bargains and 1,000 possible outcomes.

These are the actual welfare changes caused by policy bargaining when both governments' views are represented by the MCM:

| True model | Actual welfare change | |
	US	Europe
MCM	0.0002	0.0001
VAR	− 2.6394	− 2.5132
OECD	− 0.4994	0.1306
LINK	− 0.5952	0.0093

In these examples, there is at least one welfare loss whenever the 'true' models differs from the one on which the governments based their calculations before they began to bargain, even though there is no disagreement between them. That is not always the case. Both governments can gain even when both are wrong about the structure of the world economy. That happens, for example, when both governments believe that the OECD model describes the world correctly but the MCM turns out to be correct. Furthermore, they may lose more when they hold identical views than when they disagree. That happens when the MCM describes the world correctly; both parties lose when both believe in the LINK model but both gain when the US government believes in the OECD model and the European government believes in the LINK model.[64]

But the main point of the exercise is the frequency with which coordination can cause welfare losses when governments are wrong about these matters. In the 1,000 cases studied by Frankel and Rockett, the United States gains in 494, loses in 398, and is not affected significantly in the other 108, while Europe gains in 477, loses in 418, and is not significantly affected in 105. Both countries' 'failure rates' are about 40 per cent.

These are important results, but they must be interpreted cautiously. On the one hand, the models that Frankel and Rockett use may understate the governments' disagreements about economic behavior and, more importantly, the degree to which their views differ collectively from the truly 'true' model of the world economy. On the other hand, the manner in which governments are deemed to bargain may overstate the risk that they will adopt welfare-reducing policy packages.

An econometric model necessarily reflects its builders' pre-conceptions about economic behavior; they influence the selection of variables, the roles of the variables in the individual equations, and the forms of those equations. Holtham has stressed these points with particular reference to the currently popular view that economies are strongly stable in the medium term, so that fiscal and monetary policies cannot have long-lasting effects on output and employment:

How much is known about medium-term properties? The answer is not encouraging. Existing empirical models tend to fall into two groups. The models in one group started life with a short-run perspective. They often lack some of the feed-back mechanisms which are appropriate when exploring medium-run effects. The supply-side may be rudimentary with the labour-force and technical progress exogenous; stock-flow identities may be missing with no tendency for stock disequilibria to influence behaviour. Expectations may be too slow to adjust, with no tendency for agents to learn or attempt to intelligently anticipate the future. A second group of models was built for the medium term; these models have 'reasonable steady-state properties'. By this is normally meant that the models are constrained to converge on an equilibrium which has been imposed a priori; thus money is neutral, crowding out is complete etc., because these properties were objectives of the modeller.

The policy-maker wants to know about the medium-term, about issues like the probable stock of public and foreign debt consequent on policy measures. What he typically gets from empirical models is either short-run dynamics or medium-term properties that have been largely imposed. The current popularity of 'rational' expectations does not help. An a priori equilibrium is often specified in models with this assumption to serve as the basis for convergent expectations formation. That equilibrium is generally imposed on the basis of what seems reasonable from theory without empirical testing. Answers to the interesting questions (what happens in the longer run) are assumed in order to provide a basis for answering less interesting questions (how do variables behave immediately when there is 'news').[65]

Nevertheless, econometric models are forced to face the facts; they are estimated partially or completely using historical data. Frankel has pointed out that differences in view among governments may be much sharper than the cross-model differences he and Rockett have used to represent them, and he is right. We have merely to watch professional economists simplify their models when they want to solve them. They strip away 'complications' to focus on the 'main' relationships and thus come up with models that differ dramatically. Eclecticism gives way to dogmatism when tractability takes charge, and the policy makers' need for portable models – those they can carry around in their heads to analyze new information and advice – may likewise accentuate differences in view.

The other problem may be more serious, however, because it goes to the chief issue raised by the Frankel-Rockett paper, where each government is certain about its own views and equally certain about the other's views. Frankel and Rockett relax these assumptions and recalculate the governments' failure rates. In one new exercise, each government is uncertain about the other's views. Therefore, it ascribes to the other an unweighted average of the policy multipliers that come from the ten multicountry models. In another exercise, each government is uncertain about its own views as well as the other's views, so both of them use a single 'compromise' model which is, again, an average of the policy multipliers obtained from the ten models. The first exercise does not greatly affect the US failure rate but reduces the European rate to 35 per cent. The second reduces both countries' failure rates, leading Frankel to conclude that it 'offers some support for the conjecture that ministers in G-5 and Summit Meetings might do better to discuss their beliefs directly, rather than simply telling each other how they should adjust their policies'.[66]

But that is what governments have been doing all along, and there is a simple way to represent the outcome. Suppose as before that each government adheres to one of the ten models and also knows the other's model. If it is not perfectly confident about the right-ness of its views, prudential concerns should lead it to ask how a policy bargain would affect its welfare on the working supposition that the *other* government is using the right model; it should decline to strike a bargain unless it can expect to gain under *both* governments' models. If it wants to persuade the other government to accept its own proposals, an important part of the bargaining process, reputational concerns should lead it to ask how those proposals would affect the other's welfare under both governments' models. Taken together, these concerns impose a strong condition on the bargaining process. It should not get started unless each government expects to gain under *both* governments' models.

Holtham and Hughes Hallett reached the same conclusion by a slightly different route and applied this strong condition to the Frankel-Rockett bargains. They worked with six models, not ten, and had thus to analyze 36 possible bargains.[67] But they ruled out 20 of those bargains because they violated the strong condition. (There were three in which Europe would be worse off on the US view of the world, eight in which the United States would be worse off on the European view, and nine in which both would be worse off on the other's view.) This leads to the first conclusions: disagreements about economic behavior can be a major obstacle to policy-optimizing coordination because they can keep governments from getting together. But Holtham and Hughes Hallett went on to measure the welfare effects of the other 16 bargains and found that the failure rate was quite low. It was 17 per cent for the United States and the same for Europe.[68] This leads to the second conclusion: when prudential and reputational considerations block bargains that should not take place, policy coordination is not very dangerous to the participants' health.

Notes

1 Similar classifications are used by Michael Artis and Sylvia Ostry, *International Economic Policy Coordination* (Royal Institute of International Affairs and Routledge & Kegan Paul, 1986), p. 75; they cite Henry C. Wallich, 'Institutional Cooperation in the World Economy', in J. A. Frenkel and M. L. Mussa, eds., *The World Economic System: Performance and Prospects* (Dover, Mass.: Auburn House, 1984), p. 85. See also Robert D. Putnam and C. Randall Henning, 'The Bonn Summit of 1978: How Does International Economic Policy Coordination Actually Work?', Brookings Discussion Papers in International Economics, 53 (The Brookings Institution, October 1986), pp. 4–5; they cite Ralph C. Bryant, *Money and Monetary Policy in Interdependent Nations* (The Brookings Institution, 1980), pp. 477–8. But I will use 'collaboration' to describe activities that lie between 'consultation' and 'coordination', and reserve 'cooperation' to span the whole range of intergovernmental activities, including some that do not fall neatly into any of the categories discussed below. Eichengreen uses collaboration in much the same way but without distinguishing between coordination and collaboration; see Barry Eichengreen, 'International Policy Coordination in Historical Perspective: A View from the Interwar Years', in W. H. Buiter and R. C. Marston, eds., *International Economic Policy Coordination* (Cambridge University Press, 1984), pp. 140–1.

2 Cooper is exceptional in stressing the importance of exchanging information and the need for institutions to promote the process; see Richard N. Cooper, 'The Prospects for International Economic Policy Coordination', in Buiter and Marston, eds., *Policy Coordination*, p. 369. For an attempt to compare the gains from exchanging information with the gains from formal coordination, see Stephen B. Schwartz, 'The Value of Information in International Economic Policy Coordination' (unpublished manuscript, April 1987). He shows that coordination based on erroneus forecasts can be welfare-reducing, a result that resembles the finding by Frankel and Rockett concerning the effects of coordination based on erroneous views about economic behavior; see Jeffrey A. Frankel and Katherine E. Rockett, 'International Macroeconomic Policy Coordination When Policymakers Do Not Agree on the True Model', *American Economic Review*, 78 (June 1988), pp. 318–40. Schwartz also shows that the gains from exchanging information can be larger than the further gains obtained by moving from a fully informed Nash equilibrium to the corresponding Pareto equilibrium. For simulations showing the effects of informational errors on the gains from cooperative and noncooperative policies, see Andrew J. Hughes Hallett, 'Macroeconomic Policy Design with Incomplete Information: A New Argument for Co-ordinating Economic Policies', Discussion Paper 151 (Centre for Economic

Policy Research, January 1987); his work suggests that coordinated policies are less sensitive to informational errors but that the distribution of the gains from coordination may be very sensitive to those errors. For simulations showing the value of exchanging information about future policies, see Hali B. Edison and Ralph Tryon, 'An Empirical Analysis of Policy Coordination in the United States, Japan and Europe', International Finance Discussion Paper 286 (Federal Reserve Board, July 1986), where Europe and Japan are shown to gain greatly from knowing in advance what monetary policy the United States will pursue as it reduces its budget deficit.

3   Robert D. Putnam and Nicholas Bayne, *Hanging Together: Co-operation and Conflict in the Seven-Power Summits*, Revised Edition (Sage, 1987), p. 19.

4   Putnam and Bayne, *Hanging Together*, p. 19.

5   See George de Menil and Anthony M. Solomon, *Economic Summitry* (Council on Foreign Relations, 1983), and Putnam and Bayne, *Hanging Together*.

6   Bryant, *Money and Monetary Policy*, p. 465. This definition is conceptually clear but not always helpful when we try to identify actual instances of coordination. We never know what policies governments would have followed in the absence of apparent coordination. The problem arises even in the case of the 1978 Bonn summit, often described as the classic case of policy coordination. Influential groups in Germany, Japan, and the United States were urging their governments to take the very actions that they agreed to take at Bonn; those groups might have won the day even in the absence of the summit process. See Putnam and Henning, 'The Bonn Summit', who do not take this view but argue that there might have been no agreement at Bonn had those groups not been active in each country; see also Robert D. Putnam, 'Diplomacy and Domestic Politics: The Logic of Two-Level Games' (unpublished manuscript, August 1987), who argues that the 1985 Bonn summit failed to reach an agreement comparable to the 1978 agreement because there was less internal disagreement in the key countries.

7   For an interesting attempt to measure convergence within the European Monetary System (EMS), see Horst Ungerer, Owen Evans, Thomas Mayer, and Philip Young, *The European Monetary System: Recent Developments*, Occasional Paper 48 (International Monetary Fund, December 1986), ch. v; their cross-sectional regression equations explaining the behavior of national inflation rates tend to assign statistical significance to EMS membership (which they represent by a dummy variable). Using a different approach, however, I failed to find an EMS effect for the 22 industrial countries included in their sample (see Table 31). I asked whether the reduction in each country's inflation rate from 1979 to 1985 could be

explained by its initial inflation rate and a dummy variable standing for EMS membership:

$$(P_{i79} - P_{i85}) = -0.553 + 0.293 P_{i79} + 1.809 \text{ EMS}, R^2 = 0.516,$$
$$(4.47) \qquad (1.41)$$

where P_i is the rate of change in the ith country's consumer price index in 1979 or 1985, EMS is the dummy variable denoting EMS membership, and the numbers in parentheses are t statistics. The equation says that EMS countries achieved bigger reductions in inflation rates than other industrial countries but that the difference is not statistically significant. The largest reductions in inflation rates were achieved by the countries with highest rates initially, regardless of EMS membership. For more elaborate tests but equally agnostic outcomes, see Susan M. Collins, 'Inflation and the European Monetary System', in F. Giavazzi, S. Micossi, and M. Miller, *The European Monetary System* (Cambridge University Press, 1988), pp. 112–39.

8   The intervention rules of a pegged-rate regime, such as the Bretton Woods System or European Monetary System, would appear to meet these requirements, but they do not impose a clear-cut obligation to modify domestic policies, merely an obligation to intervene in the foreign-exchange market. They could be deemed to call for policy changes if they were amended to prohibit sterilized intervention, so that obligatory intervention would automatically alter the money supply; they would then become gold-standard rules, which surely qualify as policy rules. (For a stricter interpretation of the gold-standard rules, requiring central banks to reinforce the automatic money-supply changes resulting from changes in reserves, see Eichengreen, 'Coordination in Historical Perspective', pp. 139–40.)

9   I refer here to the nature of the obligations, not to the width of the band limiting exchange-rate fluctuations; for more on these ad hoc arrangements, see Kenen, *Managing Exchange Rates*, Williamson and Miller, *Targets and Indicators*, and Yoichi Funabashi, *Managing the Dollar: From the Plaza to the Louvre* (Institute for International Economics, 1988).

10   See Robert Solomon, *The International Monetary System, 1945–1981* (Harper & Row, 1982), chs. iii, v, and vii.

11   See Putnam and Bayne, *Hanging Together*, chs. 4, 6.

12   See Joseph Kraft, *The Mexican Rescue* (Group of Thirty, 1984).

13   See Sylvia Ostry, 'From Fine Tuning to Framework Setting in Macro-Economic Management', in *Opportunities and Risks for the World Economy: OECD 25th Anniversary Symposium* (Organisation for Economic Co-operation and Development, 1986), p. 17.

14   Charles P. Kindleberger, 'International Public Goods without International Government', *American Economic Review*, 76 (March 1986), p. 10.

15 Artis and Ostry, *Policy Coordination*, p. 33.

16 Artis and Ostry, *Policy Coordination*, pp. 29–30.

17 This tendency is epitomized by the communique issued at the close of the 1985 Bonn summit, which listed each government's own policy targets and said almost nothing about collective objectives. Updated versions of those lists were appended to the Plaza Communique, which did not announce new policies to drive the dollar but argued that the foreign-exchange market was taking too little account of the policies in place. The lists appended to the Louvre Accord of 1987 were slightly different; they emphasized goals rather than accomplishments. (With the notable exception of the Japanese list, however, those goals were not very new or ambitious.)

18 Putnam and Henning, 'The Bonn Summit', pp. 92–3.

19 Putnam and Henning, 'The Bonn Summit', p. 11, and Artis and Ostry, *Policy Coordination*, p. 67.

20 Putnam and Henning, 'The Bonn Summit', p. 54.

21 Putnam and Henning, 'The Bonn Summit', p. 74.

22 Artis and Ostry, *Policy Coordination*, p. 19.

23 Putnam and Henning, 'The Bonn Summit', pp. 114–15.

24 Putnam and Bayne, *Hanging Together*, p. 11.

25 Putnam and Bayne, *Hanging Together*, pp. 30–1.

26 Artis and Ostry, *Policy Coordination*, p. 70.

27 Koichi Hamada, 'Alternative Exchange Rate Systems and the Interdependence of Monetary Policies', in R. Z. Aliber, ed., *National Monetary Policies and the International Financial System* (University of Chicago Press, 1974), pp. 13–33, 'A Strategic Analysis of Monetary Interdependence', *Journal of Political Economy*, 84 (August 1976), pp. 667–700, and 'Macroeconomic Strategy and Coordination under Alternative Exchange Rates', in R. Dornbusch and J. A. Frenkel, eds., *International Economic Policy: Theory and Evidence* (Johns Hopkins University Press, 1979), pp. 292–324. Other early contributions include Richard N. Cooper, 'Macroeconomic Policy Adjustment in Interdependent Economies', *Quarterly Journal of Economics*, 83 (February 1969), pp. 1–24, Alexandre K. Swoboda, 'Policy Conflict, Inconsistent Goals, and the Co-ordination of Economic Policies', in H. G. Johnson and A. K. Swoboda, eds., *The Economics of Common Currencies* (Harvard University Press, 1973), pp. 133–42, Leif Johansen, 'The Possibility of International Equilibrium with Low Levels of Activity', *Journal of International Economics*, 13 (November 1982), pp. 257–65, Michael Jones, 'International Liquidity: A Welfare Analysis', *Quarterly Journal of Economics*, 98 (February 1983), pp. 1–23, and Matthew Canzoneri and Jo Anna Gray, 'Monetary Policy Games and the Consequences of Noncooperative Behavior', *International Economic Review*, 26 (October 1985), pp. 547–64. Useful surveys are provided by Richard N. Cooper,

'Economic Interdependence and Coordination of Economic Policies', in R. W. Jones and P. B. Kenen, eds., *Handbook of International Economics*, vol. 2 (North–Holland, 1985), ch. 23, Koichi Hamada, *The Political Economy of International Monetary Interdependence* (MIT Press, 1985), and Stanley Fischer, 'International Macroeconomic Policy Coordination', in M. Feldstein, ed., *International Economic Cooperation* (University of Chicago Press, 1988), pp. 11–43. A good introduction to the recent literature is provided by Gilles Oudiz and Jeffrey Sachs, 'International Policy Coordination in Dynamic Macroeconomic Models', in Buiter and Marston, eds., *Policy Coordination*, pp. 274–319.

28 This view of policy formation, which casts doubt on the propriety of using reaction curves, has the paradoxical consequence of supporting the use of the Nash equilibrium to represent noncooperative policy formation. Those constructs assume that each player in a strategic game believes that all other players will stand still when one player makes a move. It is therefore criticized for ruling out the 'learning by doing' that is likely to take place, not only in repeated games but even in a single, sequential adjustment process. Each player will soon see that the other players do not stand still but react to every other player's moves. If governments lump other governments' policies with 'all other things' held constant, noting perhaps that those policies change from time to time but not trying to forecast them or link them to changes in their own policies, it makes sense to assume that each government treats other governments' policies as fixed, as in the Nash equilibrium.

29 It is possible, of course, for one government to take responsibility for pegging the exchange rate (or do so unilaterally) while the others pursue domestic or collective objectives. This is the solution modeled in Canzoneri and Gray, 'Monetary Policy Games'. The Bretton Woods System is often described that way, with the United States as the country that was free to pursue a domestic or collective objective, and the EMS has been modeled that way too, with Germany replacing the United States; see, e.g., Francesco Giavazzi and Alberto Giovannini, 'Models of the EMS: Is Europe a Greater Deutschmark Area?', in R. C. Bryant and R. Portes, eds., *Global Macroeconomics: Policy Conflict and Cooperation*, (Macmillan, 1987), pp. 237–65. McKinnon's proposal for joint management of the global model supply represents a different solution to the same basic problem (see McKinnon, *An International Standard*), and his proposal is echoed by Williamson and Miller, who would use the global average of real interest rates to stabilize the global growth rate of nominal incomes (see Williamson and Miller *Targets and Indicators*). Another collective solution, involving joint intervention, is proposed in Stephen J. Turnovsky and Vasco d'Orey, 'Monetary Policies in Interdependent Economies with Stochastic Disturbances: A Strategic Approach', *Economic Journal*, 96 (September 1986), pp. 697–721. For simulations of these and other arrangements, see Warren J. McKibbin and Jeffrey D. Sachs, 'Coordination of Monetary and Fiscal Policies in the OECD', Working Paper 1800 (National Bureau of Economic Research, January 1986) and 'Comparing the Global Performance of Alternative Exchange Rate Arrangements', Brookings Discussion Papers in International Economics, 49 (The Brookings Institution, August 1986). McKibbin and Sachs examine three pegged-rate regimes: a 'dollar standard' under which the United States uses its monetary policy to pursue its domestic objectives and other countries peg their currencies to the dollar; a 'McKinnon regime' under which the sum of the national money stocks is fixed; and a 'modified McKinnon regime' under which the sum of the national money stocks is used to stabilize global nominal GNP. These are compared with four floating-rate regimes: a pure float with fixed money stocks; a noncooperative Nash regime where each government follows a money-supply rule that maximizes its own welfare function, taking other governments' policies as given; the fully cooperative counterpart of that Nash regime, involving the joint maximization of the governments' welfare functions; and a regime where each government uses its money stock to stabilize nominal GNP.

30   See the survey by Richard M. Levich, 'Empirical Studies of Exchange Rates: Price Behavior, Rate Determination and Market Efficiency', in Jones and Kenen, eds., *Handbook of International Economics*, vol. 2, ch. 19; also Robert J. Hodrick and Sanjay Srivastava, 'An Investigation of Risk and Return in Forward Foreign Exchange', *Journal of International Money and Finance*, 3 (March 1984), pp. 5–29, and 'The Covariation of Risk Premiums and Expected Future Spot Exchange Rates', *Journal of International Money and Finance*, 5 (Supplement 1986), pp. 5–21, and David A. Hsieh, 'Tests of Rational Expectations and No Risk Premium in Forward Exchange Markets', *Journal of International Economics*, 17 (August 1984), pp. 173–84.

31   For evidence that expectations are not rational, see Jeffrey A. Frankel and Kenneth A. Froot, 'Using Survey Data to Test Standard Propositions Regarding Exchange Rate Expectations', *American Economic Review*, 77 (March 1987), pp. 133–53, and Kathryn M. Dominguez, 'Are Foreign Exchange Forecasts Rational? New Evidence from Survey Data', *Economic Letters*, 21 (1986), pp. 277–81. On the peso problem, see Susan M. Collins, 'PPP and the Peso Problem' (unpublished manuscript, 1987); on the need to allow for speculative bubbles, see Wing T. Woo, 'Speculative Bubbles in the Foreign Exchange Market', Brookings Discussion Papers in International Economics, 13 (The Brookings Institution, March 1984). Frankel tried unsuccessfully to isolate the risk premium that one would expect to find when asset holders are risk averse; see Jeffrey A. Frankel, 'In Search of the Exchange Risk Premium: A Six-Currency Test Assuming Mean-Variance Optimization', *Journal of International Money and Finance*, 1 (June 1982),

pp. 255–74; but see also Jeffrey A. Frankel and Charles M. Engel, 'Do Asset-Demand Functions Optimize Over the Mean and Variance of Real Returns? A Six-Currency Test', *Journal of International Economics*, 17 (November 1984), pp. 309–23, who reject the assumption of mean-variance optimization that Frankel used to conduct his earlier search. Finally, see Hodrick and Srivastava, 'The Covariation of Risk Premiums', who find it hard to explain the erratic behavior of the realized risk premium, measured by assuming rational expectations, and Jeffrey A. Frankel and Kenneth A. Froot, 'Interpreting Tests of Forward Discount Unbiasedness Using Survey Data on Exchange Rate Expectations', Working Paper 1963 (National Bureau of Economic Research, June 1986), who use survey data to measure the risk premium but cannot do much better.

32 Maurice Obstfeld, 'Exchange Rates, Inflation, and the Sterilization Problem: Germany, 1975–1981', *European Economic Review*, 21 (March 1983), pp. 161–89, and A. Blundell-Wignall and Paul R. Masson, 'Exchange Rate Dynamics and Intervention Rules', *International Monetary Fund Staff Papers* (March 1985), pp. 132–59.

33 Kenneth Rogoff 'On the Effects of Sterilized Intervention: An Analysis of Weekly Data', *Journal of Monetary Economics*, 13 (September 1984), pp. 133–50, Bonnie E. Loopesko, 'Relationships among Exchange Rates, Intervention, and Interest Rates: An Empirical Investigation', Staff Studies, 133 (Federal Reserve Board, November 1983), and Karen K. Lewis, 'Risk Aversion and the Effectiveness of Sterilized Foreign Exchange Market Intervention', Working Paper 367 (Salomon Brothers Center for the Study of Financial Institutions, New York University, December 1985), and 'Testing for the Effectiveness of Sterilized Foreign Exchange Market Intervention Using a Structural Multilateral Asset Market Approach', Working Paper 372 (Salomon Brothers Centre for the Study of Financial Institutions, New York University, March 1986); also Kathryn M. Dominguez, 'Does Sterilized Intervention Influence Exchange Rates? A Test of the Signaling Hypothesis' (unpublished manuscript, 1986), whose results appear to say that sterilized intervention is effective when the central bank's monetary policy lends credibility to its exchange-rate policy.

34 Gilles Oudiz and Jeffrey Sachs, 'Macroeconomic Policy Coordination Among the Industrial Economies', *Brookings Papers on Economic Activity*, 1, 1984, pp. 1–64. In all such exercises, it is necessary to choose one of many cooperative solutions. It is easy to rule out solutions in which one country loses (i.e., to use the results of the initial Nash solution to impose incentive-compatibility constraints), but this does not solve the problem completely. Oudiz and Sachs solve it by using the Nash bargaining solution (not to be confused with the noncooperative Nash solution); others solve it by assuming that the bargaining process maximizes a Bergsonian welfare function in which each national welfare function is given the same weight. The precise location of the cooperative solution and the resulting distribution of welfare gains is not inconsequential for the likelihood of successful coordination: 'Every negotiation is, at its core, a zero-sum game, even there are substantial mutual gains to be had from it. If the mutual gains are obvious, the negotiators quickly take those for granted, and the bargaining immediately focuses on the distribution of gains' (Cooper, 'Prospects for Coordination', p. 371). This will be true even when policy coordination is concerned with collective goals or regime preservation; each government will still be attentive to the effects of the bargain on its own objectives and will seek to tilt the bargain in its favor. Indeed, each is bound to interpret the collective objectives in terms of its own national objectives. Putnam and Bayne quote the confidential advice that Chancellor Schmidt received on the eve of the 1978 Bonn summit:

Our economies have grown close together in recent years. For this reason, the idea of a concerted strategy among the industrialized countries has won more and more friends. If the Federal Republic takes part in such a concerted action, it does so, not out of altruism, but out of solid national interest. Given the export dependence of our economy, a higher employment level can be achieved only if our exports rise more strongly. This assumes that we put our partners in a position to import more goods from the Federal Republic. Essentially, that must happen through higher imports by the Federal Republic, and that in turn assumes that domestic demand here at home rises more sharply than is to be expected according to current trends (*Hanging Together*, pp. 89–90).

35 In another paper, however, Sachs and McKibbin use their own global (MSG) model to show that policy coordination among the industrial countries may be beneficial to the less-developed countries. It can improve their terms of trade and, more importantly, ease their debt-service burdens by reducing world interest rates; see Jeffrey Sachs and Warwick McKibbin, 'Macroeconomic Policies in the OECD and LDC External Adjustment', Discussion Paper 56 (Centre for Economic Policy Research, March 1985). The less-developed countries have been enthusiastic advocates of closer coordination among the industrial countries, focused on the growth rate of real GNP in the OECD area, on interest-rate levels, and on the stabilization of nominal exchange rates; see Deputies of the Intergovernmental Group of 24, *The Functioning and Improvement of the International Monetary System*, reprinted in *IMF Survey* (International Monetary Fund, July 1985). But I have shown elsewhere that closer coordination among industrial countries can have deleterious effects on less-developed countries when their export prices are less sticky than those of the developed countries; see Peter B.

Kenen, 'Global Policy Optimization and the Exchange Rate Regime', *Journal of Policy Modeling*, 9 (Spring 1987), pp. 19–63. (A similar effect shows up in some of the Sachs-McKibbin simulations but is swamped by the favorable interest-rate effects.)

36 Oudiz and Sachs, 'Macroeconomic Policy Coordination', p. 44.

37 Putnam and Henning, 'The Bonn Summit', p. 114.

38 See, e.g., Willem H. Buiter and Jonathan Eaton, 'Policy Decentralization and Exchange Management in Interdependent Economies', in J. S. Bhandari, ed., *Exchange Rate Management under Uncertainty* (MIT Press, 1985), p. 45, and Eichengreen, 'Coordination in Historical Perspective', p. 154.

39 Olivier J. Blanchard, 'Macroeconomic Policy Coordination among the Industrial Countries: Comment', *Brookings Papers on Economic Activity*, 1, 1984, pp. 67–8. Several recent papers have adopted Blanchard's own solution, which is to include a fiscal-balance target in the welfare function; see, e.g., McKibbin and Sachs, 'Coordination of Monetary and Fiscal Policies', and 'Comparing Alternative Exchange Rate Arrangements'.

40 Stephen N. Marris, 'Macroeconomic Policy Coordination among the Industrial Countries: Comment', *Brookings Papers on Economic Activity*, 1, 1984, p. 70.

41 Steven N. Marris, 'The Prospects for International Economic Policy Coordination', in Buiter and Marston, eds., *Policy Coordination*, p. 380.

42 Gilles Oudiz, 'European Policy Coordination: An Evaluation', *Recherches Economiques de Louvain*, 51 (December 1985), pp. 301–39. This account does not do justice to the paper, which models European interactions under various exchange-rate and leadership arrangements.

43 Matthew B. Canzoneri and Patrick Minford, 'When International Policy Coordination Matters: An Empirical Analysis', Discussion Paper 119 (Centre for Economic Policy Research, July 1986).

44 A similar point is made by Marcus Miller and Mark Salmon, 'Policy Coordination and Dynamic Games', in Buiter and Marston, eds., *Policy Coordination*, pp. 202–3, and by Frederick van der Ploeg, 'International Policy Coordination in Interdependent Monetary Economies', Discussion Paper 169 (Centre for Economic Policy Research, March 1987). Much of the theoretical and empirical literature may understate the gains from policy coordination because of the way the process is modeled. Coordination is viewed as a way to modify the path from an initial disequilibrium to a long-run equilibrium in which policy conflicts disappear (because the models usually used rule out any long-run tradeoff between unemployment and inflation). See also Matthew B. Canzoneri and Dale W. Henderson, 'Is Sovereign Policymaking Bad?' (processed, 1987), where current-account targets are used to produce permanent policy conflict and raise the gains from policy coordination.

45   Hughes Hallett, 'Macroeconomic Policy Design'.

46   Hughes Hallett, 'Macroeconomic Policy Design', Table 4 ($k = 0$). Similar results were reported in an early version of the Frankel-Rockett paper cited above; see Jeffrey A. Frankel and Katherine Rockett, 'International Macroeconomic Policy Coordination When Policy-Makers Disagree on the Model', Working Paper 2059 (National Bureau of Economic Research, 1986).

47   Gerald Holtham and Andrew J. Hughes Hallett, 'International Policy Cooperation and Model Uncertainty' in Bryant and Portes, eds., *Global Macroeconomics*, pp. 128–77.

48   Holtham and Hughes Hallett, 'International Policy Cooperation', Table 5.1. Because they use open-loop policy formation rather than dynamic programming, Holtham and Hughes Hallett must assume that policy changes are not anticipated, even when dealing with rational-expectations models, and they do not exclude time-inconsistent policy paths, Therefore, the reported gains are not strictly comparable to those obtained by other users of these models (and tend to be larger).

49   The large difference between gains obtained from RE and NRE models anticipates the result reported by Currie, Levine, and Vidalis, who find that the coordination of 'reputational' policies is unambiguously beneficial, whereas the coordination of 'nonreputational' policies leads to welfare losses. (A government pursues reputational policies when it refrains from exploiting time inconsistencies and thus keeps its word to the private sector.) In fact, it is sometimes worse to coordinate nonreputational policies than to pursue reputational policies unilaterally. See David Currie, Paul Levine, and Nic Vidalis, 'International Cooperation and Reputation in an Empirical Two-Bloc Model', in Bryant and Portes, eds., *Global Macroeconomics*, Table 4.2.

50   Kenneth Rogoff, 'Can International Monetary Policy Cooperation Be Counterproductive,' *Journal of International Economics*, 18 (May 1985), pp. 199–217. For similar cases, see Canzoneri and Gray, 'Monetary Policy Games,' van der Ploeg, 'Coordination in Interdependent Monetary Economies,' and Paul Levine and David Currie, 'The Sustainability of Optimal Cooperative Macroeconomic Policies in a Two-Country World,' Discussion Paper 102 (Centre for Economic Policy Research, April 1986). They all draw on the closed-economy case examined in Robert J. Barro and David B. Gordon, 'A Positive Theory of Monetary Policy in a Natural-Rate Model,' *Journal of Political Economy*, 91 (August 1983), pp. 589–610.

51   Taken to its logical conclusion, this argument illustrates the fundamental proposition of the 'new' macroeconomics, that monetary policy cannot affect the real economy, but it casts that proposition as a long-run tendency. If a government wants to protect its credibility, it must never try to influence output and employment by springing 'surprises' on the private sector. If a government is willing to tarnish its credibility in order to influence output and employment, it will gradually lose its ability to do so and raise the inflation rate in the process.

52 Rogoff, 'Can Policy Cooperation Be Counterproductive?' But see Currie, Levine and Vidalis, 'International Cooperation and Reputation', who show that this does not happen when governments are committed to protecting their domestic reputations (i.e., when they coordinate 'reputational' policies), and Carlo Carraro and Francesco Giavazzi, 'Can International Policy Coordination Really be Counterproductive?', Discussion Paper 258 (Centre for Economic Policy Research, 1988), who show that the problem does not arise if governments are not compelled to precommit themselves to policy coordination and can thus revert to the Nash equilibrium to 'punish' a government that breaks its promises.

53 By implication, self-contained macroeconomic models, in which a future loss of credibility is weighed against the immediate welfare gain from exploiting a time inconsistency, necessarily understate the costs of losing credibility by omitting the effects on the governments' ability to bargain in other policy domains. This point is stressed by Putnam and Henning, 'The Bonn Summit', p. 98.

54 Miller and Salmon, 'Policy Coordination and Dynamic Games', Oudiz and Sachs, 'Coordination in Dynamic Macroeconomic Models', and McKibbin and Sachs, 'Coordination of Monetary and Fiscal Policies'.

55 Levine and Currie, 'The Sustainability of Optimal Policies'. But they go on to show that the gains from coordinating fully optimal policies can probably be sustained by the threat to revert to the Nash equilibrium. Hence, governments may not try to exploit the time inconsistencies that lurk in their optimal policy plans.

56 Polly R. Allen and Peter B. Kenen, *Asset Markets, Exchange Rates, and Economic Integration* (Cambridge University Press, 1980), p. 200.

57 The same point is made by Ralph C. Bryant, 'Intergovernmental Coordination of Economic Policies: An Interim Stocktaking', in P. B. Kenen, ed., *International Monetary Cooperation: Essays in Honor of Henry C. Wallich*, Essays in International Finance, 169 (International Finance Section, Princeton University, 1987), pp. 4–15.

58 This problem is discussed more generally in Putnam and Henning, 'The Bonn Summit', pp. 104–6. They question the stability of the unitary-actor welfare function used by most economists when studying policy coordination. The welfare function is bound to change from government to government, but even more frequently than that, because of shifting bureaucratic and political alliances during the life of any single government. Economists are starting to nibble at these problems; see Guido Tabellini,

'Domestic Politics and the International Coordination of Fiscal Policies', Discussion Paper 226 (Centre for Economic Policy Research, 1988), and the sources cited there.

59   Putnam and Henning, 'The Bonn Summit', p. 100.

60   Putnam and Henning, 'The Bonn Summit', p. 100.

61   Rogoff, 'Can Policy Cooperation Be Counterproductive?'

62   Frankel and Rockett, 'Policy Coordination When Policymakers Do Not Agree', and Jeffrey A. Frankel, *Obstacles to International Macroeconomic Policy Coordination*, Princeton Studies in International Finance, 64 (International Finance Section, Princeton University, 1988).

63   Frankel and Rockett, 'Policy Coordination When Policymakers Do Not Agree', Tables 10 and 11. All other results reported below come from these two tables. They pertain to the coordination of monetary and fiscal policies, but similar results obtain when coordination is limited to monetary policies. Policy coordination is represented by the Nash bargaining solution, and the policy targets and welfare weights are those of Oudiz and Sachs (see Table 1 above).

64   This last example is important because it sheds light on the nature of the fundamental problem addressed by Frankel and Rockett. They stress the costs of disagreements among governments, but this example demonstrates that welfare losses can arise when there is no disagreement. The Frankel-Rockett results really reflect the risks of trying to coordinate policies when governments do not know how the world economy works–of ignorance rather than disagreement. In a sense, their basic point complements the warning in Vaubel, 'Coordination or Competition', that policy coordination can compound the damage done by errors in analysis or economic forecasting, giving too much weight to fashionable views.

65   Gerald Holtham, 'International Policy Coordination: How Much Consensus Is There?', Brookings Discussion Papers in International Economics, 50 (The Brookings Institution, September 1986), pp. 25–6.

66   Frankel, *Obstacles to Policy Coordination*.

67   Holtham and Hughes Hallett, 'International Policy Cooperation'. Their calculations were based on an early version of the Frankel-Rockett paper and were based on the six models for which Frankel and Rockett reported complete results–the four models mentioned above plus Patrick Minford's Liverpool Model and the McKibbin-Sachs Global Model.

68   The failure rates reported here are not strictly comparable with those reported earlier in the text, because they cover six models, not ten. (The failure rate for the 36 outcomes studied by Holtham and Hughes Hallett, obtained from the earlier version of the Frankel-Rockett paper, was about 38 per cent.) Holtham and Hughes Hallett also tell us what would happen if one government applied my 'prudential' test unilaterally. If the United States refused to bargain unless it could expect to gain under both countries' models, its failure rate would fall to 19 per cent; if Europe behaved analogously, its failure rate would fall to 21 per cent. (When both parties act this way, the strong condition applies, just as it does when both follow my 'reputational' test, and the failure rates are those reported in the text.)

Chapter 3

Policy coordination under pegged and floating exchange rates

The conventional approach

The early literature on policy coordination, including Hamada's seminal papers, dealt mainly with pegged exchange rates. Policy coordination was thought to be unnecessary if exchange rates floated freely. The need for coordination was seen to arise because every government had two policy objectives, external and internal balance, and only one policy instrument, the interest rate or money supply. With floating exchange rates, governments would not have to worry about external balance. Furthermore, floating rates would insulate each country's economy from the others' policies, relieving the governments of any need to coordinate their policies in order to achieve internal balance.

Mundell had already warned that capital mobility could interfere with insulation and had also shown that high capital mobility might resolve the target-instrument problem under pegged exchange rates; governments could use monetary policies for external balance and fiscal policies for internal balance.[1] The importance of capital mobility was not widely understood, however, and the domestic policy problem was not always seen in terms of output growth with low inflation, a formulation that poses a target-instrument problem even under floating rates.

Economists were well aware of the need to limit national autonomy under a pegged-rate regime. The regime itself imposes certain limits, especially on monetary policies, because governments truly committed to pegged exchange rates cannot neglect the balance-of-payments effects of their own policies. Those balance-of-payments effects, however, can transmit the influence of one country's policies strongly and promptly to other countries, before they have forced the offender to modify its policies. Furthermore, the balance-of-payments constraint cannot prevent concurrent or collective errors. Therefore, a pegged-rate regime cannot work well without strict limits on national autonomy and safeguards against global mismanagement – tight links between each country's money stock and its own reserves, and restrictions on the growth rate of global reserves. This was the core of the textbook case for the gold standard and the central objection to the gold-exchange standard, which allows the reserve-currency country to finance balance-of-payments deficits by creating its own reserves.

Implicit in this view, however, is the rather cynical supposition that governments will misbehave whenever possible, so that the most arbitrary limitation on the growth rate of global liquidity will be superior to unconstrained national behavior. This ranking is questionable when governments are deemed to have legitimate policy objectives, and when they have balance-of-payments or reserve-stock targets as well as domestic targets, arbitrary limits on global liquidity can lead to policy conflicts or, in game-theoretic terms, non-cooperative policy equilibria. That was the starting point for Hamada's analysis.[2]

Hamada posed the problem in a way that pointed to an obvious solution – the collective management of global liquidity to avoid worldwide inflation or deflation stemming from governments' efforts to achieve their balance-of-payments or reserve-stock targets. He did not stress policy coordination. When Eichengreen returned to the problem a decade later, he ruled out Hamada's solution. The two governments in his model were made to pursue incompatible reserve-stock targets, each wanting to hold more than half of the global gold stock. Therefore, he shifted the focus from reserve management to policy coordination.[3]

Most of the recent literature, however, takes a different tack. Instead of studying policy coordination under a pegged-rate regime, it asks whether exchange-rate pegging without additional coordination can be better than noncooperative behavior under a floating-rate regime. In other words, it asks whether exchange-rate pegging can serve as a partial or second-best substitute for policy-optimizing coordination.

The rationale for this approach is the economists' concern with reneging – the belief that governments are prone to cheat and will not engage in optimal coordination because they cannot trust each other.[4] A government cannot cheat on a firm commitment to exchange-rate pegging without being caught, and it is also possible for a single government to peg its exchange rate unilaterally, without help from any other government. Therefore, exchange-rate pegging is viewed as a viable alternative to full-fledged coordination. But its welfare effects turn out to depend on the particular model used and on the specific disturbances analyzed, which is, of course, the lesson taught by the separate but closely related literature on optimal exchange-rate management for a small economy.[5] Exchange-rate pegging is never superior to optimal policy coordination when there is no cheating, and it is not always superior to noncooperative behavior under floating exchange rates, not from a global standpoint nor from the standpoint of a single government pegging its exchange rate unilaterally. (Noncooperative behavior typically dominates pegging when the specific disturbance under study requires a change in the real exchange rate.)

There are grave objections to this way of comparing exchange-rate regimes and to the models used. First, the approach itself attaches excessive importance to the problem of reneging. The obstacles to policy-optimizing coordination make it worth considering second-best arrangements, but cheating is not the most important obstacle, and some of the others, including uncertainty about the future and about the structure of the world economy, would interfere with policy optimization even under pegged exchange rates. Second, the literature focuses too heavily on the limiting case of perfect capital mobility, with the consequences mentioned in the previous chapter. With perfect capital mobility, exchange-rate pegging is necessarily viewed as an alternative to policy coordination, rather than a framework for coordination, because governments cannot peg their exchange rates and pursue other objectives simultaneously. It is therefore impossible to deal with the questions posed at the start of this book: How do exchange-rate arrangements affect the demand for policy co-ordination? How do they affect the conduct of coordination and its welfare effects?

A different framework

The history of policy coordination says that it is rather rare. There have been many instances of regime-preserving cooperation but very few instances of mutual policy adjustment. The summit countries have been trying to design a framework for more systematic cooperation in macroeconomic matters, which is perhaps starting to influence policy formation. But they have not shown that they are willing or able to conduct their monetary and fiscal policies in keeping with mutually agreed objectives or to adopt policy rules that would limit their autonomy. They can perhaps agree to engage in damage limitation – to avoid or rectify serious mistakes in designing and conducting their national policies – and that would be a striking achievement. They cannot be expected to go much farther. It is therefore worth asking whether there are ways to minimize the need for close coordination, paying particular attention to exchange-rate arrangements.

A conventional two-country model can shed light on this issue. Its main features are described below, and complete solutions are supplied in the appendix to this book. It will be used to show how each government will modify its monetary policy when faced by exogenous shocks or policy changes in the other country. Certain shocks and policies will drive the two economies into suboptimal situations; the governments will fall short of reaching their domestic targets, and policy coordination can help to minimize the shortfall.

It will also be shown, however, that exchange-rate arrangements strongly affect the need for coordination. Shocks that produce suboptimal situations under a floating exchange rate will not always do so under a pegged rate, which will therefore permit each government to reach its domestic targets by independent, decentralized changes in its monetary policy. As governments are bound to have more trouble making decisions collectively than separately, arrangements that maximize the scope for decentralized decision making can be said to dominate other arrangements. Therefore, this model leads to an unusual conclusion. Because pegged exchange rates are less likely to produce suboptimal situations from which governments must extract themselves collectively, pegged exchange rates can be said to dominate floating rates.

I drew this same general conclusion in an earlier paper, which used a different model.[6] The model was more general in some respects, because the two economies under study were not completely symmetrical in structure or behavior. Furthermore, it included a third country designed to represent the less-developed countries, to study the effects of shocks coming from that country and show how policy coordination among the developed countries affects the less-developed countries. The less-developed countries do not always benefit from policy coordination, contrary to the commonly expressed view that they are hurt by deficient coordination and to the Sachs-McKibbin result that they would be the biggest gainers from more coordination among the developed countries.[7] That model was less general in other ways, however, because the velocity of money was fixed, preventing certain disturbances from affecting inflation rates and thus circumscribing the effects of fiscal policies. Furthermore, it did not examine the implications of 'negative transmission' in the floating-rate case. The analysis that follows, moreover, extends the argument in two directions.

First, it makes an important point about fiscal policies. The output and price effects of a fiscal disturbance cannot be offset fully by monetary policies. Under a pegged exchange rate, however, one country can adjust its fiscal policy to neutralize fully the spillover effects of the other's fiscal policy, and this is impossible under a floating rate. Second, it shows that a once-for-all change in a pegged exchange rate can be combined with changes in monetary policies to neutralize the output and price effects of a switch in demand between the countries' goods, a disturbance that cannot be offset fully under rigidly pegged or freely floating rates. In other words, collective management of the exchange rate can facilitate the decentralized management of monetary policies.

The case for exchange-rate pegging that comes from this analysis needs to be qualified carefully. The analysis deals with well-behaved economies that travel automatically to long-run equilibrium after they encounter an exogenous shock, and it deals with well-behaved governments that do not try to block that process but are interested only in choosing the best path to the new equilibrium. The potential for policy conflict is thus transient, not permanent, and the analysis may understate the gains from policy coordination.[8] Furthermore, each government trusts its partner to behave sensibly – to accept the inevitability of the long-run equilibrium in which output and employment come to rest at their 'natural' levels, rather than try to manipulate them. It is not concerned to insulate itself from bad behavior by its partner or limit its partner's independence by controlling the stock of reserves. On the contrary, the supply of reserves is infinitely elastic.[9] In brief, the two governments behave cooperatively, not antagonistically, in every conceivable way, including the choice and management of a pegged exchange rate. This is unrealistic, but so is the opposite view. Repeating a point made earlier, the use of game-theoretic methods to analyze policy interdependence should not lead us to assume that governments are like oligopolists vying for markets or profits.

The model also neglects some issues stressed in other recent studies. The private sector does not have forward-looking expectations, which means that it cannot anticipate disturbances or the governments' policy reactions to them, and it does not connect current with future fiscal policies. And though the private sector is risk averse, it pays no attention to the different implications of pegged and floating exchange rates for the variability of nominal returns on assets denominated in different currencies.[10] Finally, the governments' policy reactions are once-for-all open-market operations, which may not fully optimize the paths of their economies, and governments do not learn from experience. The policy game is static, not dynamic.[11]

This presentation has three parts. The first lays out the model and imposes some simplifications. The second is concerned with extracting the governments' reaction curves, showing how exchange-rate arrangements affect them, and showing how various disturbances shift them. The third is devoted to the main question – how pegged and floating exchange rates affect the demand for policy coordination when governments want to optimize the process of adjustment after their economies have been disturbed by a permanent shock. It deals thoroughly with one disturbance, because it can be analyzed diagrammatically, but discusses other shocks and policy changes that are treated algebraically in the appendix.

The model

There are two countries, the US and EC, which are identical in size and behave symmetrically. Their currencies are the dollar and ecu, respectively. Each country supplies one good, one bond, and one currency. The goods and bonds are traded and are imperfect substitutes, but the currencies are held only by the residents of the issuing countries.

Asset markets and goods markets clear continuously, but goods prices are sticky. An increase in the demand for the US good, for example, does not raise its price immediately. There is instead a temporary increase in US output that reduces unemployment below its long-run or 'natural' level. But wages and prices start to rise in response to the increase in output and go on rising until output and unemployment return to their natural levels. US bonds are dollar bonds issued by the US government when it runs a budget deficit. EC bonds are ecu bonds issued by the EC government. The two countries' money supplies are managed by their central banks, using open-market operations in their own bond markets. When the dollar-ecu exchange rate is pegged, however, money supplies can be affected by central-bank intervention in the foreign-exchange market, because intervention is not necessarily sterilized.

Expectations are static, as was indicated earlier, and the model begins in long-run equilibrium, where there is no saving or investment, budgets and trade flows are balanced, and unemployment stands at its natural level so that wages and prices are stationary. When the situation is disturbed, moreover, each economy moves gradually to a new long-run equilibrium, driven by changes in wealth induced by transitory saving and, with floating exchange rates, by capital gains and losses on holdings of foreign-currency bonds. As governments are well behaved, they do not try to manipulate their economies. Therefore, they may be said to begin at the 'bliss points' defined by their social welfare functions, and the two countries' bliss points will coincide. This means, in turn, that the Nash or noncooperative solution to the model coincides with the Pareto or cooperative solution, and there is no scope for policy coordination in long-run equilibrium.

When this situation is disturbed, however, each government must act to minimize the welfare loss caused by the resulting output and price changes. But there are two classes of disturbances. Some disturbances can be shown to shift both bliss points together, so that the Nash and Pareto solutions continue to coincide, and there is no need for policy coordination. Each government can use its monetary policy to neutralize completely the output and price effects of the disturbance and can thus move directly to its new bliss point, forestalling any welfare loss. Other disturbances can be shown to shift the bliss points differently, so that the Nash and Pareto solutions cease to coincide, and monetary policies cannot be expected to neutralize completely the output and price effects of those disturbances. Each government must settle for a second-best result, involving a departure from its bliss point and a welfare loss, and policy coordination is needed to minimize the loss.

The model is written in dollar terms. All nominal variables are dollar-denominated except those with primes and those pertaining to the EC bond (F, F^c, etc.), which are ecu-denominated. When helpful in avoiding ambiguities, the subscripts 1 and 2 are used to denote US and EC variables, respectively, while asterisks denote long-run values (and changes in certain desired values when different from actual values).

The US economy
As the two economies are fully symmetrical, I will describe the US
economy completely and can then describe the EC economy
succinctly. The equations for the US economy are listed in Table 2.

Table 2 *The US economy*

---

(1) $W_1 = L_1 + B_1 + \pi F_1$

(2) $(dW_1/dt) = S_1 + F_1(d\pi/dt)$

(3) $L_1 = B^c - R$

(4) $B = B_1 + B_2 + B^c$

(5) $(dB/dt) = g(B^* - B), 0 < g < 1$

(6) $g(B^* - B) = G_1 + r_1 B - T_1 - T_{12} - r_1 B^c, T_{12} = r_1 B_2 - r_2 \pi F_1$

(7) $L_1 = (1/v)\exp[-\delta(r_1 - \tilde{r})]p_1 Q_1, \delta > 0$

(8) $\pi F_1 = \beta_1 \exp[-\tfrac{1}{2}\phi(r_1 - r_2)]W_1, 0 < \beta_1 < 1, \phi > 0$

(9) $S_1 = s(W_1^* - W_1), 0 < s < 1$

(10) $W_1^* = \alpha \exp[\theta \ (r_1 - \tilde{r})]Y_1^d, 0 < s \alpha < 1, 0 < \theta < \phi$

(11) $Y_1^d = p_1 Q_1 + r_1 B_1 + r_2 \pi F_1 - T_1 = p_1 Q_1 - G_1 + g(B^* - B)$

(12) $p_1 c_{11} = (1 - a_1)(Y_1^d - S_1 + G_1), p_2 c_{21} = a_1(Y_1^d - S_1 + G_1)$

(13) $q_1 = p_1^{1-a_1} p_2^{a_1}$

(14) $Q_1 = c_{11} + c_{12}$

US households hold three assets, US money, US bonds, and EC
bonds, so that US wealth is given by equation 1, in which W_1 is US
wealth measured in dollars, L_1 and B_1 measure US holdings of US
money and bonds, F_1 measures US holdings of EC bonds in ecu, and
π is the exchange rate in dollars per ecu. (An increase in π is a
depreciation of the dollar.) The time path of US wealth is given by
equation 2, in which S_1 is US saving, and the second term in the
equation measures the capital gain conferred by a depreciation of the
dollar, which raises the dollar value of EC bonds held by US
residents.

The US money supply is defined by equation 3. It is equal to the
central bank's holdings of US bonds, B^c, less the dollar value of its

reserve liabilities to the EC central bank, R. An increase in B^c represents an open-market purchase by the US central bank; an increase in R represents nonsterilized intervention in the foreign-exchange market (a dollar purchase by the EC central bank to keep the dollar from depreciating). It also measures a balance-of-payments surplus for the EC and deficit for the US.

The supply of dollar bonds, B, is fixed at any point in time; it can change only gradually as the US government runs a budget deficit or surplus. Equation 4 is the market-clearing equation for the US bond, in which B_1 and B_2 are the quantities held by US and EC residents and B^c is the quantity held by the US central bank. The evolution of B is given by equation 5, which is a stylized representation of fiscal policy. The government chooses a target level of debt, B^*, and runs a budget deficit or surplus until target and actual debt levels are equal. The government cuts taxes to run a deficit, then rescinds the tax cut gradually to satisfy equation 5. (Note that the coefficient g has no subscript, which says that it will be the same in the US and EC. This is also true of coefficients appearing in equations 7 through to 10 below.)

Equation 6 is the US budget equation, in which G_1 is the government's spending on US and EC goods, r_1 and r_2 are the interest rates on the US and EC bonds, T_1 is the lump-sum tax that the government adjusts continuously to achieve the desired surplus or deficit, and T_{12} is an intergovernmental transfer payment from the EC to the US that serves to remove all interest-income terms from the definitions of the current-account balance and disposable income.[12] A change in G_1 should be regarded as a balanced-budget change in government spending; once B^* is chosen, determining the budget surplus or deficit, any change in G_1 must be offset by a change in T_1 to keep it from affecting the surplus or deficit.

The demand for US money by US households is given by equation 7. It is a standard specification in which the transactions demand for money is defined with respect to the value of domestic output (Q_1 is the volume of US output and p_1 is its dollar price) but depends on the interest rate too; the demand for money falls when r_1 rises above $\tilde{r}$, its initial level. (The demand for US money should be made to depend on

r_2 as well as r_1, because US residents hold EC bonds, but that link is omitted for simplicity; the same objection can be raised against equation 10, below, defining desired wealth.) The US demand for the EC bond is given by equation 8. When interest rates are the same in the two countries, US holdings are a constant fraction β_1 of US wealth, but that fraction rises when the interest differential moves in favor of the EC bond. The US demand for the US bond is given residually by equations 1, 7, and 8.

Equation 9 makes the level of saving depend on the difference between desired and actual wealth, and equation 10 makes desired wealth depend on the domestic interest rate and disposable income, Y_1^d. The term $s\alpha$ is the marginal propensity to save out of disposable income, which is why it must lie between zero and unity. The restriction on θ puts a lower bound on capital mobility. Disposable income is given by equation 11 (with a transformation that uses equation 6 to replace the lump-sum tax T_1).

Households and the government have the same preferences with regard to goods, and a_1 measures the share of the EC good in total spending by US households and the US government. These assumptions are used in equations 12 to define the levels of US spending on the US and EC goods; c_{11} is the quantity of the US good consumed by US households and the US government, c_{21} is the corresponding quantity of the EC good, and p_2 is the dollar price of the EC good. Equation 13 uses these assumptions to define the US consumer price index.

Finally, equation 14 is the market-clearing equation for the US good, in which c_{12} is the quantity imported by the EC for household and government consumption.

The EC economy

Some of the EC equations are shown in Table 3. Equation 1' and 2', for EC wealth, are basically the same as their US counterparts but look rather different because they are written in terms of the foreign currency (i.e., in dollars rather than ecu). In these equations, W_2 is EC wealth measured in dollars, L_2' and F_2 measure holdings of EC money and bonds in ecu, B_2 measures holdings of US bonds in dollars, and S_2 is EC saving measured in dollars.

Table 3 The EC economy

(1')	$W_2' = \pi(L_2' + F_2') + B_2$
(2')	$(dW_2/dt) = S_2 + (L_2' + F_2)(d\pi/dt)$
(3')	$L_2' = F^c + (1/\pi)R$
(4')	$F = F_1 + F_2 + F^c$
(5')	$(dF/dt) = g(F^* - F)$
(6')	$g(F^* - F) = G_2' + r_2F - T_2' + (1/\pi)T_{12} - r_2F^c$
(7')	$L_2 = (1/v)\exp[-\delta(r_2 - \tilde{r})]p_2Q_2$
(8')	$B_2 = \beta_2 \exp[\tfrac{1}{2}\phi(r_1 - r_2)]W_2,\ 0 < \beta_2 < 1$

The supplies of the two EC assets are given by equations 3', 4', and 5', where F^c, F, and F^* play the same roles that B^c, B, and B^* played in the corresponding US equations. (As R will be initialized at zero and will not change thereafter unless the exchange rate is pegged, there is no need to put a valuation term in equation 3' to keep capital gains and losses on dollar-denominated reserves from affecting the EC money supply inappropriately.) Equation 6' is the EC budget equation and is written in ecu for clarity; the terms G_2' and T_2' play the same roles that G_1 and T_1 played in the US budget equation. The demand for EC money and the EC demand for the US bond are given by equations 7' and 8', and the EC demand for the EC bond is defined residually.

The remaining equations for the EC economy, defining saving, desired wealth, disposable income, the levels of EC spending on the two goods, and the consumer price index, are identical to their US counterparts, equations 9 through 13, apart from subscripts. The market-clearing equation for the EC good is omitted because it is made redundant by Walras' Law.

Strategic simplifications
Four conditions are imposed on the initial situation. All prices are normalized at unity ($p_1 = p_2' = \pi = 1$, so that $p_2 = \pi p_2' = 1$, and $q_1 = q_2 = \pi q_2' = 1$). Outputs, interest rates, and levels of government spending are equal in the two countries ($Q_1 = Q_2 = Q$, $r_1 = r_2 = \tilde{r}$,

and $G_1 = G_2' = G$). The two economies begin in a stationary state ($S_1 = S_2 = 0$, $B = B^*$, and $F = F^*$), so trade must be balanced initially. Under these conditions, moreover, levels of wealth are equal initially ($W_1 = W_2 = W$), and $a_1 = (1 - a_2) = a$, where a_1 and a_2 are the shares of the EC good in US and EC consumption, respectively. Finally, net reserves are zero ($R = 0$).

Two additional restrictions are imposed on economic behavior. (1) Each country's consumption is biased toward its own home good, so that $0 < a < \frac{1}{2}$.[13] (2) Whenever $r_1 = r_2$, the share of the foreign-currency asset in each country's wealth is equal to the share of the imported good in that country's consumption, so that $\beta_1 = \beta_2 = a$.[14] On this assumption, moreover, $B = \pi F = W$ initially.

The model is solved for the short-run and long-run effects of six disturbances: open-market purchases of the domestic bond in the US and EC; a permanent shift by US or EC households from the EC bond to the US bond; a permanent shift in US or EC expenditure from the US good to the EC good; temporary tax cuts in the US and EC causing permanent increases in stocks of debt; permanent increases of government spending in the US and EC matched by increases in lump-sum taxes; and permanent increases in desired wealth causing temporary increases in saving.[15] As prices are sticky in both countries, they are held at unity to obtain the short-run solutions, but outputs are allowed to vary. As outputs return to their natural levels eventually, they are held at their initial levels to obtain the long-run solutions, but prices are allowed to vary.

The short-run and long-run solutions for both pegged and floating exchange rates are shown in the appendix. The main short-run results are summarized in Table 4, and the main long-run results in Table 5. (The two fiscal disturbances are combined in Table 4, because they have the same-signed short-run effects.)

None of the results will be surprising to readers familiar with recent literature on the international transmission of disturbances, but two of them deserve an additional word. (1) The floating-rate results in both tables depend on an assumption made in the appendix that capital mobility is high enough to cause the 'negative transmission' of monetary policies. A monetary expansion in one country depresses

Table 4 *Short-run effects of exogenous disturbances and policy changes*

Effect on	Open-market purchase in US*	Switch in demand to US bond	Switch in demand to EC good	Fiscal expansion in US*	Increase in desired US wealth*
Pegged rate:					
Reserves**	+	−	+	−	+
US output	+	+	−	+	−
EC output	+	−	+	?	?
Floating rate:					
Exchange rate**	+	−	+	−	+
US output	+	−	−	+	−
EC output	−	+	+	+	−

*The effects of the corresponding EC disturbance are symmetrical to those of the US disturbance; the signs of the reserve and exchange-rate changes are reversed, and the signs of the US and EC output changes switch positions.
**Positive entries denote increases in EC reserves in the pegged-rate case and appreciations of the ecu (depreciations of the dollar) in the floating-rate case.

Table 5 *Long-run effects of exogenous disturbances and policy changes*

Effect on	Open-market purchase in US*	Switch in demand to US bond	Switch in demand to EC good	Increase in US government spending*	Increase in US US tax cut*	Increase in desired US wealth*
Pegged rate:						
Reserves**	+	−	+	+	+	−
Price indexes:						
US (in dollars)	+	0	−	+	+	−
EC (in ecu)	+	0	+	+	+	−
Floating rate:						
Exchange rate**	+	−	+	+	+	−
Price indexes:						
US (in dollars)	+	−	+	+	+	−
EC (in ecu)	−	+	−	+	?	−

*The effects of the corresponding EC disturbance are symmetrical to those of the US disturbance; the signs of the reserve and exchange-rate changes are reversed, and the signs of the US and EC output changes switch positions.
**Positive entries denote increases in EC reserves in the pegged-rate case and appreciations of the ecu (depreciations of the dollar) in the floating-rate case.

the other country's output in the short run and depresses its price level in the long run; the other country's currency appreciates strongly, and the expenditure-switching and expenditure-reducing effects of the appreciation are large enough to swamp the expenditure-raising effects of lower interest rates in both countries. (2) This assumption is not strong enough, however, to resolve some other ambiguities: under a pegged exchange rate, fiscal expansion in one country can raise or lower output temporarily in the other country; under a floating rate, one form of fiscal expansion (a temporary tax cut) can raise or lower the price level permanently in the other country.

The policy reaction curves

Recall what was said about the two governments. They do not try to keep output and employment above or below their natural levels, and they do not try to prevent their economies from returning to long-run equilibrium whenever they are driven from it. Nevertheless, they have well-defined preferences regarding the paths their economies should follow as they return to long-run equilibrium. Those paths are represented here by the short-run change in output and permanent change in the price level, with the latter standing for the inflation or deflation that occurs on the way to the new equilibrium. This use of comparative-static changes in outputs and price levels permits a two-dimensional representation of the whole adjustment process.

Depicting Preferences and Drawing Reaction Curves
The preferences of the US government are represented by the indifference curve in Figure 1, where movements along the horizontal axis measure short-run changes in US output (deviations from its long-run level) and movements along the vertical axis measure permanent changes in the US price level (deviations from unity). The origin thus represents the initial long-run equilibrium and also represents the peak or 'bliss point' of the indifference map; all departures from that long-run equilibrium are deemed to reduce economic welfare. The indifference curves need not be symmetrical around the origin,

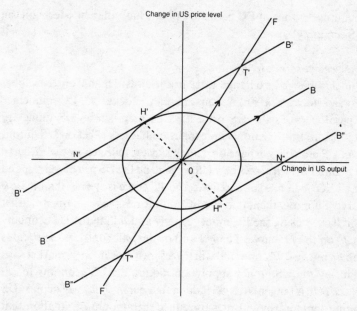

Figure 1

because the government can detest inflation more than deflation and an output loss more than an output gain. Furthermore, the US indifference map can differ from the EC map. But both must have their bliss points at the origin when governments do not try to drive their economies away from the initial situation.[16]

The indifference map in Figure 1 can be used to derive a reaction curve for the US government, showing how it will alter US monetary policy in response to a change in EC monetary policy. The derivation makes use of the *BB* curve, which shows how an open-market purchase by the US authorities affects US output in the short run and the US price level in the long run. Tables 4 and 5 show that the *BB* curve has the same basic properties under pegged and floating exchange rates; an open-market purchase raises US output temporarily and raises the US price level permanently. Therefore, it moves the US economy upward along the *BB* curve. But the government's reaction curve has different properties under the two exchange-rate regimes, because a change in EC monetary policy has different effects on the US economy.

The pegged-rate case

Under a pegged exchange rate, price levels depend on the global money stock, not on national money stocks, so EC monetary expansion raises the US price level by as much as US monetary expansion. But EC monetary expansion has less effect on US output than US monetary expansion, and this fact is reflected by the *FF* curve in Figure 1, which shows how US output and the US price level respond to an EC open-market purchase. The *FF* curve is steeper than the *BB* curve. Suppose, then, that the EC authorities make an open-market purchase, raising the EC money supply and taking the US economy to *T'* on the *FF* curve. The US authorities will confront the options shown by the *B'B'* curve and will therefore make an open-market sale, reducing the US money supply and taking the US economy to *H'*, where *B'B'* is tangent to a US indifference curve. They will depress US output temporarily in order to reduce the amount of inflation that occurs as the US economy moves to a new long-run equilibrium.

The US price level is higher at *H'* than it was initially, however, which means that the US open-market sale was smaller than the EC open-market purchase. Therefore, the US reaction curve must look like I_1 in Figure 2, where the horizontal axis measures the quantity of dollar bonds held by the US central bank and the vertical axis measures the quantity of ecu bonds held by the EC central bank. The slope of the US reaction curve depends on the shape of the US indifference map in Figure 1. It is in fact the counterpart of the curve *H'H''* in Figure 1, which is the locus of tangencies between the family of *BB* curves and the US indifference curves. But I_1 is always steeper than a 45° line.

Let *P* in Figure 2 represent the initial situation, before any change in US or EC monetary policies, so that it corresponds to the origin in Figure 1. It is therefore the US bliss point, and a new set of US indifference curves can be drawn around it. They will be ellipses and will have a special property; they will be horizontal at their intersections with US reaction curve.[17]

An EC reaction curve can be derived in precisely the same way and is represented by I_2 in Figure 2. It is necessarily flatter than a 45° line, and P is the EC bliss point as well as the US bliss point, because both economies start in long-run equilibrium. An EC indifference map could therefore be drawn around P, with curves that would be vertical at their intersections with the EC reaction curve. By implication, P describes a very special situation. Suppose that the US authorities choose B^c on the (Nash) supposition that the EC authorities will not alter F^c and that the EC authorities behave analogously. The two countries will wind up in Nash equilibrium at P, but this equilibrium will not be suboptimal, even though the governments are not cooperating, because it is the bliss point for both of them.

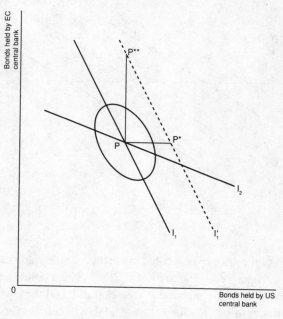

Figure 2

Before looking at policy reactions under a floating exchange rate, let us see how various shocks affect the positions of the pegged-rate reaction curves and the locations of the corresponding bliss points.

Consider Figure 3, which reproduces the *BB*, *FF*, and *H'H''* curves. Suppose that a permanent shock takes the US economy to *D**, which lies on *BB*. If allowed to work its way through the economy, it would depress output temporarily and reduce the price level permanently. But an open-market purchase by the US central bank could take the US economy directly to its long-run equilibrium without any change

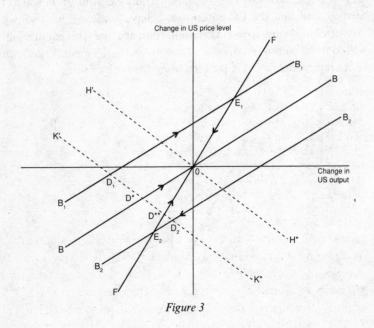

Figure 3

in output or the price level; it could move the economy along *BB* from *D** to the origin. Returning to Figure 2, the US bliss point shifts from *P* to *P**, where *B^c* is higher and *F^c* is unchanged, and the US reaction curve shifts from I_1 to I_1'. Suppose instead that the shock takes the US economy to *D***, which lies on *FF*. An open-market purchase by the EC central bank could take the US economy directly to its long-run equilibrium, moving it along *FF* from *D*** to the origin. In this case, then, the US bliss point shifts from *P* to *P***, where *B^c* is unchanged and *F^c* is higher, and the US reaction curve shift to I_1' once again.

Generalizing from these special cases, any disturbance that takes the US economy to a point on a line such as $K'K''$ in Figure 3, beneath $H'H''$ but parallel to it, will shift the US reaction curve outward, but the location of the new US bliss point will depend on the precise characteristics of the disturbance:

(1) If it takes the economy to a point such as D_1, above D^*, the economy can move directly to long-run equilibrium if the US authorities make an open-market purchase and the EC authorities make an open-market sale; the US purchase will move the economy upward along B_1B_1 from D_1 to E_1, and the EC sale will move it downward along FF from E_1 to the origin. In Figure 2, the new US bliss point will lie to the southeast of P^*.

(2) If it takes the economy to a point such as D_2 below D^{**}, the economy can move directly to long-run equilibrium if the US authorities make an open-market sale and the EC authorities make an open-market purchase; the US sale will move the economy downward along B_2B_2 to E_2, and the EC purchase will move it upward along FF from E_2 to the origin. In Figure 2, the new US bliss point will lie to the northwest of P^{**}.

(3) If it takes the economy to a point between D^* and D^{**}, in the region bounded by the BB and FF curves, the economy can move directly to long-run equilibrium if both countries' authorities make open-market purchases. In Figure 2, the new US bliss point will lie between P^* and P^{**}.

It should perhaps be noted that the processes described above as returning the economy to the origin in Figure 3 can also be described as changing the coordinates of that origin. That is how they are depicted in Figure 2, where they shift the US bliss point and the whole US indifference map. By implication, a disturbance that takes the US economy to a point on $H'H''$ can be deemed to shift the coordinates in Figure 3 and thus shift the bliss point in Figure 2 but without shifting the US reaction curve (since $H'H''$ is the counterpart of the original reaction curve).

To see how a disturbance can create the need for policy co-ordination, consider a disturbance that has identical effects on the US and EC economies. Let them begin at the common bliss point P in Figure 4, where the original reaction curves (not shown) would intersect, and let the disturbance take them to points such as D_1 in Figure 2. The US reaction curve will shift outward to I_1' in Figure 4, and the new US bliss point will be P_1, where B^c would rise and F^c

would not change. The EC reaction curve will shift outward to I_2', and the new EC bliss point will be P_2, where F^c would rise and B^c would not change. Each government would like to make an open-market purchase but wants the other to do nothing, so there is intrinsic conflict between them.

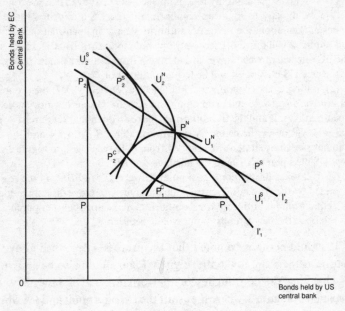

Figure 4

The noncooperative equilibrium would be established at P^N where the new reaction curves intersect, and this outcome is suboptimal, because both governments fail to reach their bliss points. Each is obliged to choose the best available path to long-run equilibrium (strictly speaking, the best available starting point), given the choice made by the other.[18] Fully cooperative equilibria would be established on the so-called contract curve connecting the two countries' bliss points and passing through points such as P_1^C and P_2^C, which are points of tangency between pairs of indifference curves. To reach such points, however, the governments must coordinate their policies; they must agree to a package of policy changes or follow appropriate policy rules, because they will not depart unilaterally from the Nash equilibrium.

Interpreting cooperative equilibrium

The cooperative equilibria in Figure 4 have three important characteristics:

First, some of them are clearly superior to the Nash equilibrium, but others are not. Suppose that the US government was forced to choose between the Nash equilibrium and a form of policy coordination which would lead it to a point on the contract curve between P_2 and P_2^C and thus to an indifference curve lower than U_1^N, which passes through P^N. It would prefer the Nash equilibrium and reject coordination. Similarly, the EC government would reject coordination which took it to a point on the contract curve between P_1 and P_1^C and thus to an indifference curve lower than U_2^N. In the language of game theory, the only incentive-compatible cooperative solutions are those that lie between P_2^C and P_1^C. It may be possible to devise institutional arrangements or policy rules that produce incentive-compatible solutions, but they must be robust, in that they must function appropriately for various disturbances, because every disturbance leads to a different policy configuration. This point illustrates Rogoff's observation that game theory should lead us to think about modifying institutions rather than particular policies.[19]

Second, policy coordination cannot take two economies directly to their long-run equilibria, because it cannot take both of them to their bliss points. Coordination does not obviate the need for gradual adjustment; it merely helps governments to choose better paths, given their policy preferences. Policy coordination is second-best in principle to exchange-rate and other institutional arrangements that remove the intrinsic conflict between governments' objective, and coordination may be second-best in practice because policy and rules cannot be expected to produce solutions that lie exactly on the contract curve or, if they do, to reach it in a timely manner.

Third, the gains from policy coordination depend on the particular characteristics of the shocks that produce the need for coordination.

Those characteristics determine the shifts in the reaction curves and bliss points, and the bliss-point shifts are crucial. Suppose that the disturbance illustrated in Figure 4 had shifted the reaction curves as shown but had shifted the bliss points differently. Let P_1 and P_2 move closer to P^N, taking the contract curve with them and shrinking the incentive-compatible segment (the one bounded by P_1^C and P_2^C). There will be less scope for policy coordination, and the welfare gains will get smaller. Taking this argument to its limit, let the disturbance move both bliss points directly to P^N. There will be no need for policy coordination, because the Nash and cooperative equilibria will coincide, just as they did initially. Each government, acting independently, can use its monetary policy to take its economy directly to its long-run equilibrium, forestalling the need for gradual adjustment and avoiding any welfare loss.

This limiting case is not a curiosity. It is, indeed, the basis for the main conclusion drawn in this chapter. A pegged exchange rate dominates a floating rate because it can cause the countries' bliss points to shift together, permitting fully optimal policy responses without any need for coordination.

Two more equilibria are shown in Figure 4. They are the Stackelberg equilibria in which one country leads and the other follows, and they have been used extensively to represent and analyze hegemonic situations, such as UK leadership before 1914 and in the interwar period and US leadership under the Bretton Woods system.[20] I have reservations about these ways of using them; the models from which they are extracted are not rich enough to account for the emergence, maintenance, or gradual decline of hegemonic power. They deserve brief treatment here, however, because they shed light on the problem of incentive compatibility and the difficulty of devising cooperative arrangements under a floating-rate regime.

The Stackelberg solution with US leadership is shown at P_1^S in Figure 4. Having watched the policy responses of the EC authorities and studied their pronouncements, the US authorities know the shape and position of the EC reaction curve. Therefore, they can set their monetary instrument, B^c, to establish an equilibrium at P_1^S, where the US indifference curve U_1^S is tangent to the EC reaction curve. Because that indifference curve intersects the US reaction curve between the Nash point P^N and the US bliss point P_1, US leadership is better from the US standpoint than the Nash equilibrium. It is worse from the EC standpoint, however, because P_1^S lies beyond P^N on the EC reaction curve and is therefore farther from the EC bliss point. If the EC was able to exercise leadership, we would be examining the point P_2^S, and the welfare orderings would be reversed. The EC would be better off than in the Nash and the US would be worse off.[21]

The main point of interest here, however, has to do with incentive-compatible cooperation when the Stackelberg, not Nash, is taken as the starting point, and Figure 4 highlights the issues. If the US can expect to achieve and maintain Stackelberg leadership, it will not agree to policy coordination unless it is promised a point on the contract curve lying between P_1^C and P_1.[22] Outcomes that were incentive compatible when the Nash was taken as the starting point are not incentive compatible when the Stackelberg is taken as the starting point. This does not rule out policy coordination, because points acceptable to the US will also be acceptable to the EC. If we were to draw the EC indifference curve passing through P_1^S, it would cut the contract curve below P_1^C, carving out a subset of cooperative solutions that are welfare improving for both countries. But the set of incentive-compatible bargains is sharply skewed in favor of the US, compared to the set that corresponded to the Nash equilibrium. Analogous problems arise when the EC is able to assert Stackelberg leadership.

The floating-rate case

Under a floating exchange rate, price levels depend on national money stocks, not on the global money stock, and they are affected directly by exchange-rate changes, because the home-currency prices of imported goods appear in each country's price index. For these and other reasons, the reaction curves look and behave quite differently under a floating rate. The *BB* curve in Figure 1 has the same basic properties under floating and pegged exchange rates (although its slope can differ), and an open-market purchase by the US central bank drives the US economy upward along the *BB* curve. But the properties of the *FF* curve are different with a floating rate. Tables 4 and 5 show that monetary expansion in the EC reduces US output temporarily and reduces the US price level permanently. Hence, the *FF* curve will still be upward sloping, but an open-market purchase by the EC central bank will drive the US economy downward. Furthermore, the *FF* curve can be flatter or steeper than the *BB* curve, depending on the relative strengths of various output and price effects.

Returning to Figure 1 and beginning at the origin, consider the effects of an EC open-market purchase. It will take the US economy to a point such as *T″* and induce the US authorities to make an open-market purchase to take their economy to *H″*, where the *B″B″* curve is tangent to the US indifference curve. It can be shown that the US open-market purchase will be smaller than the EC open-market purchase, which means that the US reaction curve will look like I_1 in Figure 5. It will be steeper than a 45° line, just like it was before, but

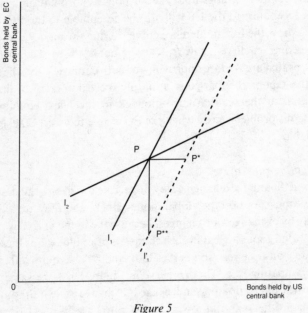

Figure 5

positively sloped, not negatively sloped. This is the main result of 'negative transmission' under a floating exchange rate. The EC reaction curve can be derived in the same way and will look like I_2.

How do shocks affect the position of the US reaction curve and the location of the US bliss point? Returning to Figure 3, we begin again with a disturbance that takes the US economy to D^*. The US authorities can neutralize the shock completely by making an open-market purchase to take the US economy back to the origin along the BB curve. In Figure 5, then, the US reaction curve shifts outward from I_1 to I_1', and the US bliss point moves from P to P^*, where B^c has risen but F^c has not changed. Nothing new thus far. But let us look next at a disturbance that takes the US economy to D^{**}. The EC authorities can neutralize the shock completely by making an open-market sale to take the US economy back to the origin along the FF curve. The US reaction curve shifts to I_1', as before, but the US bliss point shifts to P^{**}, where F^c has fallen but B^c has not changed. We can therefore identify three classes of cases:

(1) If a disturbance takes the US economy to a point such as D_1, above D^*, the economy can move directly to long-run equilibrium if both central banks make open-market purchases. The US purchase will take the economy upward along BB from D_1 to E_1, and the EC purchase will take it downward along FF from E_1 to the origin. In Figure 5, the new US bliss point will lie to the northeast of P^*.

(2) If a disturbance takes the US economy to a point such as D_2, below D^{**}, the economy can move directly to long-run equilibrium if both central banks make open-market sales. The US sale will take the economy downward along BB from D_2 to E_2, and the EC sale will take it upward along FF from E_2 to the origin. In Figure 5, the new US bliss point will lie to the southwest of P^{**}.

(3) If a disturbance takes the US economy to a point between D^* and D^{**}, the economy can move directly to long-run equilibrium if the US authorities make an open-market purchase and the EC authorities make an open-market sale. In Figure 5, the new US bliss point will lie between PP and P^{**}.

Figure 6 is the floating-rate counterpart of Figure 4, showing how a particular disturbance affects the policy equilibrium between the US and EC. As before, we start in long-run equilibrium at P and examine the effects of a permanent disturbance that takes both economies to

D^* in Figure 1. The US reaction curve shifts outward to I_1' and the US bliss point shifts to P_1; the EC reaction curve shifts outward to I_2' and the EC bliss point shifts to P_2. Each country would like to make an open-market purchase but wants the other to do nothing, just as in the pegged-rate case.

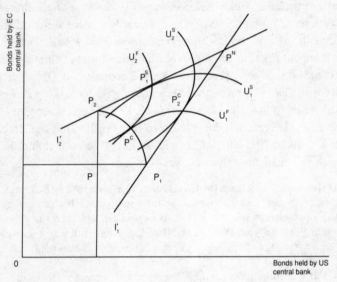

Figure 6

The Nash equilibrium is at P^N and the set of fully cooperative equilibria lie on the contract curve connecting the two bliss points (P^C is one such equilibrium). Thus far, then, the outcomes resemble those in Figure 4 for the pegged-rate case, even though the reaction curves are positively sloped. But there are two major differences.

First, there is a larger set of incentive-compatible cooperative solutions, because the Nash solution lies farther from the contract curve. The set includes the whole segment of the contract curve that would be bounded by indifference curves drawn from P^N. (That segment is longer than the segment bounded by the curves U_1^S and U_2^S, because the indifference curves drawn from P^N would necessarily lie outside those curves.)

Second, the Stackelberg solutions are quite different. If the US acts as leader, the Stackelberg equilibrium will be at P_2^S and will raise the leader's welfare. The relevant US indifference curve, U_1^S, cuts the US reaction curve between P^N and the US bliss point. But US leadership is also good for the EC, because the corresponding EC indifference curve, U_2^F, cuts the EC reaction curve between P^N and the EC bliss point. In fact, it is better to follow than lead. The EC indifference curve that corresponds to EC leadership, U_2^S, cuts the EC reaction curve between P^N and P_1^S and is thus lower than U_2^F.

If both governments try to be followers, they are likely to lapse back into the Nash equilibrium, which is the worst outcome in the floating-rate case. But another possibility is more interesting. If both governments believe that they can be followers, they may refuse to engage in any form of policy coordination. That is the outcome illustrated in Figure 6, where the followers' indifference curves, U_1^F and U_2^F, have been drawn to be tangent at P^C, so there are no incentive-compatible cooperative outcomes (and matters could be even worse, because there could be a gap between the points at which the followers' indifference curves intersect the contract curve). With floating exchange rates, then, each government will want the other to lead, so that it can follow, and both governments may shy away from policy coordination.[23] If both governments see the Nash equilibrium as the most likely consequence of noncooperation, there may be more scope for policy coordination with floating than with pegged rates. If both governments hope to be Stackelberg followers, there may be little or no scope for coordination.

Disturbances, bliss-point shifts, and the ranking of exchange-rate regimes

Having asked how hypothetical disturbances will shift the countries' bliss points under alternative exchange-rate arrangements, let us go on to look at actual disturbances – the five featured in the model. We begin with one that is easy to illustrate.

A switch in demand between bonds

Suppose that portfolio preferences change. US or EC households decide to substitute dollar bonds for ecu bonds. Tables 4 and 5 show that this shift raises US reserves under a pegged exchange rate and causes the dollar to appreciate under a floating exchange. Under a pegged rate, moreover, it raises US output temporarily and reduces EC output but does not have any permanent effect on the two countries' price levels. Under a floating rate, by contrast, it reduces US output, raises EC output, and does have permanent effects on price levels. The appreciation of the dollar, which is largely responsible for reducing US output, reduces the US price level by reducing the dollar price of the imported good. The depreciation of the ecu, which is largely responsible for raising EC output, raises the EC price level by raising the ecu price of the imported good.

The pegged-rate effects of this disturbance are represented in Figure 1. US output rises temporarily by ON'', EC output falls by ON', and those two distances are equal. Hence, the shift in the US bliss point corresponds to a downward movement along $B''B''$ from N'' to T'' and an upward movement along FF from T'' to the origin. The effects of the disturbance on the US economy can be completely neutralized if the US authorities make an open-market sale and the EC authorities make an open-market purchase. The shift in the EC bliss point corresponds to an upward movement along $B'B'$ from N' to T' and a downward movement along FF from T' to the origin. The effects on the EC economy can be neutralized if the EC authorities make an open-market purchase and the US authorities make an open-market sale. It is easily shown, moreover, that the US open-market sale needed to return the US economy to long-run equilibrium is precisely the one needed by the EC economy, while the EC open-market purchase needed to return the EC economy to long-run equilibrium is the one needed by the US economy. The two countries' bliss points shift together, and the new non co-operative equilibrium is fully optimal. There is no need for policy coordination.

The open-market operations needed in this instance are those which sterilize the change in reserves produced by the shift in bondholders' preferences. If EC bondholders want to buy more US bonds and must thus buy dollars in the foreign-exchange market, the US authorities must sell dollars and buy ecu to defend the exchange rate, and their intervention will raise the US money supply if nothing else is done. Therefore, the US authorities must sell dollar bonds to stabilize the US money supply, and this sale furnishes the extra dollar bonds that EC bondholders want to hold. In the EC, meanwhile, the authorities must prevent the EC money supply from falling in response to the US intervention in the foreign-exchange market, so they must buy ecu bonds, and their purchase absorbs the ecu bonds that EC bondholders no longer want to hold.[24]

The floating-rate effects of the switch in demand for bonds reduce US output and the US price level, moving the US economy to a point in the southwest quadrant of Figure 1, and the point lies above the *FF* curve. The disturbance raises EC output and the EC price level, moving the EC economy to a point in the northeast quadrant, and the point lies below the *FF* curve. But it is hard to locate these points precisely in relation to the countries' *BB* curves (and the *BB* curves can be steeper or flatter than the *FF* curves in the floating-rate case). Therefore, it is hard to describe the bliss-point shifts geometrically.

The algebraic results are unambiguous, however, in saying that the bliss points do not shift together. Decentralized changes in monetary policies cannot neutralize completely the effects of the shift in bondholders' preferences, and governments must be content to optimize the subsequent adjustment process. Furthermore, the paths they will choose independently in the new Nash equilibrium are inferior to those they can choose collectively by policy co-ordination. The situation looks like the one in Figure 6, where the Nash equilibrium is clearly inferior to a set of incentive-compatible cooperative equilibria. Therefore, this case is one in which a pegged exchange rate dominates a floating rate, not only because it obviates the need for policy coordination but also because the best result obtainable under a floating rate, even with coordination, is inferior to the result obtainable under a pegged rate.

Shifts in fiscal policies

Throughout this book, changes in fiscal policies are treated as part of the problem rather than part of the solution; they are deemed to occur for extraneous reasons, not for macroeconomic reasons, and monetary policies are used to offset their output and price effects. Two fiscal-policy changes are examined here: balanced-budget changes in government spending and temporary changes in lump-sum taxes that raise or reduce supplies of debt. The effects of the former, moreover, are virtually identical to the effects of a permanent decrease in desired wealth, resulting in a temporary decrease in saving and an increase in consumption. Let us start with that disturbance.

Consider the output and price effects of a balanced-budget increase in US government spending (the effects of an increase in EC spending are symmetrical). According to Tables 4 and 5, US output rises in the short run under a pegged exchange rate, EC output can rise or fall, and both countries' price levels rise permanently. The effects are too complicated to illustrate diagrammatically, but the algebraic outcomes are clear. The US and EC bliss points shift together, allowing the two governments, acting independently, to neutralize the output and price effects of the disturbance. (The US authorities must make an open-market sale, and the EC authorities must make an open-market purchase.) There is no need for policy coordination. Under a floating exchange rate, both countries' outputs rise temporarily, and their price levels rise permanently. There are no ambiguities. Nevertheless, the countries' bliss points do not shift together. Therefore, we have two more cases in which a pegged rate dominates a floating rate – the fiscal disturbance itself and its private-sector counterpart, a permanent decrease in desired wealth.

The effects of a temporary tax cut are more complicated than most others, because its short-run and long-run effects differ fundamentally. A tax cut acts mainly on goods markets in the short run, by raising disposable incomes and the demands for goods, and its impact depends on its size. (Its short-run asset-market effects come chiefly from the influence of income changes on the demand for money.) But a tax cut acts mainly on asset markets in the long run, by raising the supply of debt, and its impact depends on its duration as well as its size. In other words, its long-run effects depend partly on the speed-of-adjustment coefficient, g, in equation 6 of Table 2.

Consider the effects of a US tax cut (the effects of an EC tax cut are symmetrical). Turning again to Tables 4 and 5, we find the same ambiguity with regard to the temporary change in EC output under a pegged exchange rates but an additional ambiguity with regard to the permanent change in the EC price level under a floating rate. Furthermore, the bliss-point shifts depend in part on the speed-of-adjustment coefficient. Under a pegged exchange rate, the two countries' bliss points shift together in one special case, where $(1 - s\alpha)g = s$, but not in any other instance, and they never shift together under a floating rate. Therefore, a pegged rate cannot be said to dominate a floating rate.

Yet pegged rates have an advantageous feature. Suppose that the EC authorities, facing the effects of a US tax cut, raise EC taxes and run a budget surplus that offsets exactly the US budget deficit. They reduce the EC debt target, F^*, to offset the increase in the US target, B^*, and choose the same speed-of-adjustment coefficient. As each country's tax policy affects its own output more strongly than foreign output and also affects its price level more strongly, the two countries' fiscal policies act jointly to raise US output and the US price level and to reduce EC output and the EC price level. The US authorities can then make an open-market sale, the EC authorities can make an open-market purchase, and these additional policy measures will take their economies to a common bliss point. Furthermore, those measures can be taken without explicit coordination; the two governments have merely to exchange information, so that the EC authorities can forecast the path of the US budget deficit. Comparable adjustments are not possible, however, under a floating rate, even when governments exchange information. Once again, own effects dominate cross effects, output and the price level rise in the US and fall in the EC when the US runs a budget deficit and the EC runs a surplus. But the requisite changes in monetary policies do not take the two economies to a common bliss point.[25]

A switch in demand between goods

Consider the effects of a switch in demand from the US good to the EC good. Under a pegged exchange rate, US output falls temporarily and the US price level falls permanently, while EC output rises temporarily and the EC price level rises permanently. Under a floating exchange rate, the signs of the output changes are the same but those of the price-level changes are reversed by the depreciation of the dollar; the US price level rises and the EC price level falls. Yet the countries move to different bliss points under both regimes, so one regime does not dominate the other.

In this case too, however, a pegged rate is advantageous, because a once-for-all devaluation of the dollar can be combined with open-market operations to bring the two economies to a common bliss point. The devaluation is chosen to neutralize completely the price-level effects of the switch in demand, which means that the governments have merely to deal with the output effects of the switch in demand modified by those of the devaluation. The situation is much like the first one discussed in this section and illustrated in Figure 1, where a switch in demand between bonds raised one country's output and reduced the other's by the same amount, and the solution is just like that one. One central bank must make an open-market purchase, the other must make an identical open-market sale, and the two economies will move to the same bliss point.

Conclusion

The exercise presented above leads to a strong and novel conclusion. There is more scope for decentralized policy formation under pegged exchange rates than under floating rates, which do not give governments more freedom to choose their policy objectives and do not insulate their economies from external shocks or the effects of other countries' policies. Pegged rates do not reduce structural interdependence. Nevertheless, they reduce the demand for policy coordination by allowing governments to neutralize completely the effects of certain shocks without having to strike bargains with each other.

This conclusion is not robust or general enough to make a compelling case for returning to pegged exchange rates. Too many restrictive assumptions were used to produce it. Economies were well behaved, in that they began in long-run equilibria where wages and prices were constant and returned to those equilibria when they were driven from them, so that permanent disturbances did not have permanent effects on outputs or inflation rates. Governments were well behaved, in that they did not try to drive their economies away from their long-run equilibria and did not pursue incompatible objectives, such as current-account surpluses, and they had enough confidence in their partners' integrity to give them open-ended access to reserves. Assets were imperfect substitutes, so that sterilized intervention could influence exchange rates and monetary policies could be used to pursue other policy targets. Furthermore, the economies behaved symmetrically and were equal in size, and the analysis dealt with a rather short list of disturbances, paying no attention to supply shocks.

Yet the conclusion is strong enough to play some part in any comprehensive comparison between pegged and floating exchange rates. It is important to know that floating rates may intensify rather than reduce the need to coordinate national policies, and to know the reason. It is partly because of the familiar complaint against floating exchange rates, that changes in nominal exchange rates resulting from asset-market shocks and shifts in expectations interact with sticky prices to change real exchange rates, and partly because of the tendency for floating rates to destabilize domestic price levels by changing the home-currency prices of imported goods.

The same conclusion can be put in different terms. The case for policy coordination is frequently made by appealing to the need for exchange-rate stabilization to prevent oscillations in real exchange rates. That is the usual and most compelling rationale for exchange-rate stabilization.[27] The case made here, however, treats exchange-rate stabilization as a way to reduce the need for governments to coordinate their policies in order to achieve their own objectives – as a framework for maximizing welfare rather than a welfare-maximizing target.

Two more conclusions should be noted, although they are quite familiar. First, large changes in fiscal policies are hard to handle, but harder to handle with floating exchange rates. Hence, policy coordination must aim at the avoidance of such changes and at prompt rectification of fiscal mistakes. Fiscal policies can play an important role in macroeconomic stabilization; they should be part of the solution, not part of the problem. But they can become a big part of the problem when tax cuts are inspired by doctrinaire notions about economic behavior or used to shrink the public sector by starving it of revenue. These experiments can be very costly, not only for the countries that conduct them but for other countries too.

Second, pegged exchange rates should not be defended rigidly. When a disturbance calls for a permanent change in relative prices, as was the case above with a switch in demand between US and EC goods, a once-for-all change in the nominal exchange rate can greatly facilitate adjustment. It is admittedly hard for governments to persuade the foreign-exchange market that they really mean to stabilize exchange rates when the market knows that there will be occasional realignments. Credibility is precious and easily squandered. But this is not to argue against exchange-rate pegging. It is to argue instead for giving governments adequate access to reserves. That is the main lesson taught by the recent literature on exchange-rate crises.[28] Central banks need deep pockets.

Earlier parts of this paper examined the aims and methods of policy coordination. Instances of true coordination have been rare, and more frequent but looser forms of cooperation have aimed mainly at damage limitation – coping with crises and preserving institutional arrangements. Governments are working on a framework that could eventually produce closer, more formal coordination, but it is too soon to know how it will evolve.

The new system was born at the Versailles summit of 1982, when the G-5 governments agreed to cooperate closely with the IMF in its surveillance of national policies. It was given more structure at the Tokyo summit of 1986, when responsibility was reassigned from the

G-5 to the G-7, and the participating governments agreed 'to review their individual economic objectives and forecasts collectively at least once a year . . . with a particular view to examining their mutual compatibility' and to base this review on a list of quantitative indicators. It was refined again at the Venice summit of 1987, when the list of indicators was pruned to six (growth rates of real GNP, inflation rates, interest rates, budget balances, trade balances, and exchange rates) and the aims of the exercise were stated more clearly. Attention was finally given to the need for governments to agree on policy objectives before they can appraise economic performance.[29] The Venice summit affirmed:

The commitment by each country to develop medium-term objectives and projections for its economy, and for the group to develop objectives and projections, that are mutually consistent both individually and collectively; and

The use of performance indicators to review and assess current economic trends and to determine whether there are significant deviations from an intended course that require consideration of remedial actions.

At this juncture, however, governments are still concerned with damage limitation – with the need for *consistent* policy objectives rather than the *quality* of those objectives. The pursuit of inconsistent objectives can cause large exchange-rate and current-account movements of the sort that have dominated recent history. But consistency should not be achieved at the expense of quality. It makes little sense to stabilize exchange rates by meshing monetary and fiscal policies in ways that sacrifice satisfactory growth rates.

Governments should be more ambitious. They should try to agree on policy norms or targets that are both sustainable and satisfactory from a global standpoint – on a target for the growth rate of global GNP, for instance, that does not stultify the growth rate of world trade and inhibit the expansion of LDC exports. It would be foolish to state such targets too precisely or revise them frequently. Much can be said for adopting a medium-term framework but making mid-course corrections in targets or instruments when actual performance proves to be inadequate or an unexpected shock assails the system. Uncertainty about economic behavior does not argue for inaction or rigid adherence to an unconditional policy rule; it is not harder to predict the effects of discretionary policy changes than to predict the effects of staying with a preannounced policy in a changing world.[30]

As for the political acceptability of a medium-term framework, Holtham has this to say:

[It] is beginning to look as if policy-makers have a more medium-term orientation than economists usually credit them with and policies are often the consequences of what is asserted by economists about the medium-term. A common economists' view of politicians is that they are essentially trying to buy votes. They can do this by delivering low unemployment and low inflation. If the voters are myopic or forgetful, politicians can win elections by inflating the economy just before the polls, reaping the temporary benefit of low unemployment and paying the inflation price later.

This view was probably always a travesty of political decision-making in most countries. Now it is quite inappropriate. In recent years politicians in at least half a dozen countries have shown more resistance than most economists to the allurements of reflation. . . . In fact, a better model of political behaviour may be that politicians act on their conception of the way that the economy works in the medium to long term and ignore shorter run dynamics as too uncertain, and unexploitable given delays in data collection and inside lags in policy-making.

The making of bargains about medium-term targets must involve politicians, which provides a role for summit meetings. Heads of government should not be expected to quantify policy targets, any more than they should be expected to draft an arms-control treaty. But they are the only ones who can mobilize domestic political support for international agreements endorsing global policy targets and assigning specific obligations to individual governments. The road to the summit must be built carefully, however, much as the road to the first Bonn summit was planned and paved by a year of meetings. I have described this elsewhere as a two-stage process:

The first stage should articulate and quantify composite policy objectives for the major industrial countries, relating to growth rates, inflation rates, and other variables. These should be framed as medium-term targets, but they should be updated and extended periodically. No attempt should be made to 'fine tune' the world, but the major industrial countries should not be allowed to pretend that they have no influence on – or responsibility for – the evolution of the world economy.

The second stage should translate the composite targets into operational commitments on the part of each participating government. Each country's obligations must be framed to take account of that country's special problems, but they should be consistent in two senses: (1) they should be adequate, taken together, to achieve the composite policy objectives; and (2) they should not involve larger changes in exchange rates than any other set of policy commitments capable of reaching the same objectives. Implementation of the policy commitments should be monitored collectively . . . in order to facilitate reciprocal adjustments whenever the need becomes apparent.

Implicit in this passage and central to my view is the need for governments to frame their commitments in terms of their policy instruments, rather than the mixture of targets and instruments currently used by the G-7 governments. It is doubly dangerous to monitor and coordinate policies by focusing directly on targets. It introduces long lags into the process, because judgments about the appropriateness of national policies must await the arrival of the relevant data, and it opens the way for governments to avoid responsibility by blaming events beyond their control when they do not meet their targets.[33]

Any such system calls for careful monitoring, and it makes sense to look at both instruments and targets when assessing economic performance. Assessments must be made frequently, moreover, using global and national forecasts, as well as the most recent data. Emerging gaps between targets and outcomes must be spotted quickly to diagnose policy errors and the arrival of new shocks. Bargains about global targets and national instruments should be made in a medium-term framework and not altered frequently. Nevertheless, the need for change must be detected promptly, in time to plan the next bargain carefully.

There is still need for damage limitation and 'peer pressure' to correct policy mistakes, and it may be unrealistic to call for more strenuous efforts. Fischer may be reading history rightly when he concludes that 'there would be little need for coordination if each country were taking good care of its own domestic policies'.[34] Yet the

recent performance of the world economy calls for something more –
for commonly agreed policy adjustments to extricate the world
economy from policy mistakes that have not yet been rectified and
from the damaging side-effects of having to correct them tardily.

Notes

1   Robert A. Mundell, *International Economics* (Macmillan, 1968), chs.
11, 16; see also Peter B. Kenen, 'Macroeconomic Theory and Policy: How the
Closed Economy Was Opened', in Jones and Kenen, eds., *Handbook of
International Economics*, vol. 2, ch. 13.

2   Koichi Hamada, 'A Strategic Analysis of Monetary Independence',
Journal of Political Economy, 84 (August 1976). See also Michael Jones,
'International Liquidity: A Welfare Analysis', *Quarterly Journal of Economics*, 98 (February 1983), pp. 1–23 where a reserve constraint on each
individual government can produce a Pareto-superior policy equilibrium in
the absence of explicit coordination; the constraints reduce the spillover
effects of monetary policies aimed at stabilizing domestic output.

3   Barry Eichengreen 'International Coordination in Historical Perspective: A View from the Interwar Years', in W. H. Buiter and R. C. Marston,
eds., *International Economic Policy Coordination* (Cambridge University
Press, 1984). Policy coordination does not allow the governments to reach
their incompatible reserve targets but keeps them from imposing deflation on
each other as they pursue those targets.

4   See, e.g., Matthew Canzoneri and Jo Anna Gray, 'Monetary Policy
Games and the Consequences of Noncooperative Behavior', *International
Economic Review*, 26 (October 1985), pp. 547–64.

5   See the citations in note 1 to Chapter 1, especially the Roper-
Turnovsky and Frenkel-Aizenman papers.

6   Peter B. Kenen, 'Global Policy Optimization and the Exchange Rate
Regime', *Journal of Policy Modeling*, 9 (Spring 1987), pp. 19–63. See also
Peter B. Kenen and John D. Montgomery, 'Global Policy Optimization and
the Exchange-Rate Regime: Dynamic Stability and Parametric Sensitivity',
Working Paper G-86-03 (International Finance Section, Princeton University,
November 1986), which showed that the model was stable and leads me to
believe that the present model is also stable. (It should be noted, however,
that the earlier model did not converge monotonically. There were big
transitory changes in price levels even when there were no permanent
changes. This result limits the validity of the device used below, where long-
run comparative-static changes in price levels are used to represent the
inflationary process.)

7 Jeffrey Sachs and Warwick McKibbin, 'Macroeconomic Policies in the OECD and LDC External Adjustment', Discussion Paper 56 (Centre for Economic Policy Research, 1985).

8 The same criticism has been leveled at other models used to evaluate the benefits of policy coordination; see, e.g, Frederick van der Ploeg, 'International Policy Coordination in Interdependent Monetary Economies', Discussion Paper 169 (Centre for Economic Policy Research, March 1987).

9 This supposition is not utterly unrealistic. Members of the EMS have unlimited access to the very short-term financing facility (VSTF) of the European Monetary Cooperation Fund, which may be one reason why speculative pressures have not overwhelmed the pegged-rate arrangements of the EMS. But drawings on the VSTF must be repaid or funded, and those in the model are not subject to that limitation. On the EMS arrangements, see Stefano Micossi, 'The Intervention and Financing Mechanisms of the EMS and the Role of the ECU', Banca Nazionale del Lavoro, *Quarterly Review*, 155 (December 1985), pp. 327–45.

10 For two quite different treatments of the linkage between current and future fiscal policies, see Willem Buiter, 'Fiscal Policy in Open Interdependent Economies', in A. Razin and E. Sadka, eds., *Economic Policy in Theory and Practice* (St Martins Press, 1987), pp. 101–44, and Jacob A. Frenkel and Assaf Razin, 'Government Spending, Debt, and International Economic Interdependence', *Economic Journal*, 95 (September 1985), pp. 619–36. On the linkage between the exchange-rate regime and asset-market behavior by risk-averse agents, see Stanley W. Black, 'The Effect of Alternative Intervention Policies on the Variability of Exchange Rates: The Harrod Effect', in J. S. Bhandari, ed., *Exchange Rate Management under Uncertainty* (MIT Press, 1985), pp. 73–82, and Walter Enders and Harvey E. Lapan, 'On the Relationship Between the Exchange Regime and the Portfolio Rules of Optimizing Agents', *Journal of International Economics*, 15 (November 1983), pp. 199–224. It would be possible to simulate but not solve a perfect-foresight version of the model, but other expectational assumptions could be used, such as the assumption of long-run perfect foresight used in Rudiger Dornbusch, 'Expectations and Exchange Rate Dynamics', *Journal of Political Economy*, 84 (December 1976), pp. 1161–76, and in Polly R. Allen and Peter B. Kenen, *Asset Markets, Exchange Rates and Economic Integration* (Cambridge University Press, 1980), ch. 9 (where we call it hyperopic foresight).

11 These two simplifications are less troubling than those made with regard to private-sector behavior. That is because I am chiefly concerned to identify cases in which policy coordination is not needed, not to describe the bargains made when it is required. I am looking for cases in which once-for-all policy changes, made independently, can offset exogenous disturbances completely, obviating the need for a series of policy measures and for a bargain about them. In technical terms used below, I seek to identify cases in which once-for-all policy changes can take both governments back to their bliss points. Other economists have suggested or used this approach. See Willem H. Buiter and Jonathan Eaton, 'Policy Decentralization and Exchange Management in Interdependent Economies', in Bhandari, ed., *Exchange Rate Management*, p. 45, who show that the Nash and Pareto equilibria are both bliss-point equilibria when policy targets and instruments are equal in number; Francesco Giavazzi and Alberto Giovannini, 'Monetary Policy Interactions under Managed Exchange Rates,' Discussion Paper 123 (Centre for Economic Policy Research, August 1986), p. 15, who anticipate my approach to the ranking of exchange-rate regimes but do not carry it out; and Stephen J. Turnovsky and Vasco d'Orey, 'Monetary Policies in Interdependent Economies with Stochastic Disturbances: A Strategic Approach', *Economic Journal*, 96 (December 1986), pp. 703–4, who adopt the same strategy but deal exclusively with temporary rather than permanent shocks. Some of my conclusions have also been anticipated by Daniel Lasker, 'International Cooperation and Exchange Rate Stabilization', *Journal of International Economics*, 21 (August 1986), pp. 151–64. His argument is hard to follow, but he appears to be saying that floating exchange rates can exacerbate rather than relieve the target-instrument problem; by changing the prices of imported goods, they make it more difficult for monetary policy to stabilize domestic output without also destabilizing the price level. That is one way to interpret some of my results.

12 The same simplification is used in Allen and Kenen, *Asset Markets*, ch. 2. The final term in equation 6 is the central bank's interest income on holdings of US bonds, which is paid over to the government.

13 When the shares of imports are constant, the price elasticities of demand for imports are unity and the Marshall-Lerner-Robinson condition is satisfied. When the shares are also smaller than unity, the sum of the marginal propensities to import is smaller than unity. These conditions are imposed on most open-economy models.

14 In the language of portfolio-balance theory, asset holders choose the minimum-variance portfolio when there is no difference between expected returns on foreign and domestic assets (and expectations are static in this model, so expected returns are equal when interest rates are equal). Furthermore, the conditions $\beta_i = a < \frac{1}{2}$ say that the minimum-variance portfolio is characterized by a preference for home-currency assets; each country's holdings of the foreign-currency bond are smaller than its total holdings of home-currency assets. On the decomposition of asset holdings into minimum-variance and speculative portfolios and the connection between preferences for home goods and preferences for home assets, see

William H. Branson and Dale W. Henderson, 'The Specification and Influence of Asset Markets', in Jones and Kenen, eds., *Handbook of International Economics*, vol. 2, pp. 794–98, and Arminio Fraga, 'Price Uncertainty and the Exchange-Rate Risk Premium', *Journal of International Economics*, 20 (February 1986), pp. 179–85.

15 The effects of a balanced-budget change in government spending are identical but opposite in sign to the effects of a change in desired wealth. Hence, the mathematical appendix shows only the effects of increases in G_1 and G_2, but they should be read to stand for the effects of decreases in $W_1{}^*$ and $W_2{}^*$. For proof of the equivalence, see Peter B. Kenen, 'Exchange Rates and Policy Coordination in an Asymmetrical Model', Discussion Paper 240 (Centre for Economic Policy Research, May 1988).

16 The indifference map illustrated in Figure 1 corresponds to the quadratic welfare function commonly found in the literature. For a fuller discussion of that welfare function and the use of comparative-static output and price changes to represent the whole adjustment process, see Kenen, 'Global Policy Optimization', pp. 45–6.

17 See, e.g., Richard N. Cooper, 'Economic Interdependence and Coordination of Economic Policies', in Jones and Kenen, eds., *Handbook of International Economics*, vol. 2, pp. 1216–17. If the US and EC governments had the same preferences, their reaction curves would be symmetrical around a 45° line drawn through P.

18 The plausibility of this outcome is widely challenged in the literature, because the sequential adjustments in B^c and F^c required to reach it will show both governments that they are wasting information. Each government makes its moves on the assumption that the other will stand pat but will quickly see that the other is responding. This discovery is ruled out by assuming that governments do not learn from experience. But a better way to rationalize the Nash equilibrium was proposed earlier in the text. If each government watches its own target variables (the temporary output change and permanent price-level change), rather than the other's policy variable, and makes its own moves to reduce discrepancies between the predicted and desired values of those variables, it will not start to question the logic of its own behavior. On this view, the governments' reaction curves represent policy interdependence but depict decentralized policy formation rather than interactive behavior.

19 Kenneth Rogoff, 'International Coordination in Dynamic Macro-economic Models: Comment', in Buiter and Marston, eds., *Policy Coordination*, p. 329. Rogoff credits Hamada, 'A Strategic Analysis', with making the same point.

20 See Barry Eichengreen, 'Conducting the International Orchestra: The Bank of England and Strategic Interdependence under the Classical Gold Standard', *Brookings Discussion Papers in International Economics*, 43

(The Brookings Institution, March 1986); this is one of the few papers in which the underlying model is asymmetrical enough to explain the emergence of hegemony, answering the criticism in the text below. But Eichengreen has not stressed the crucial asymmetries. He begins with an interesting discussion of Triffin's thesis that the balance-of-payments adjustment process was fundamentally asymmetrical in the Nineteenth Century but abandons that phenomenon to focus instead on the implications of an interest-elastic official demand for reserve-currency balances. For Triffin's thesis, see Robert Triffin, 'National Central Banking and the International Economy', in *Postwar Economic Studies* (Federal Reserve Board, 1947), pp. 59–62; also Peter B. Kenen, *British Monetary Policy and the Balance of Payments, 1951–1957* (Harvard University Press, 1960), pp. 56–63.

21　There is no way to stop a government from trying to be a leader; it has merely to set and hold its policy instrument (B^c or F^c) at the appropriate level. But the other government will not want to follow in the situation described by Figure 4, and it can make matters difficult for a would-be leader by concealing or falsifying information about its own policy reactions. Under a floating exchange rate, however, it may be best to follow.

22　The point P_1^C happens to be the tangency between U_1^S and U_2^N, but that is coincidental. (It is convenient, however, because it separates neatly the two sets of incentive-compatible cooperative outcomes. Those defined with reference to the Nash equilibrium lie to the northwest of P_1^C, and those defined with reference to US Stackelberg leadership lie to the southeast of it.)

23　See Cooper, 'Economic Interdependence', pp. 1217–18; related points are made by Eichengreen, 'Coordination in Historical Perspective', pp. 162–3, and 'Conducting the International Orchestra', pp. 17–18.

24　These are familiar results; see Peter B. Kenen, 'Effects of Intervention and Sterilization in the Short Run and the Long Run', in R. N. Cooper, P. B. Kenen, J. B. de Macedo, and J. van Ypersele, eds., *The International Monetary System under Flexible Exchange Rates* (Ballinger, 1982), pp. 64–5, and Dale W. Henderson, 'Exchange Market Intervention Operations: Their Role in Financial Policy and Their Effects', in J. F. O. Bilson and R. C. Marston, eds., *Exchange Rate Theory and Practice* (University of Chicago Press, 1984), pp. 370–1. To use Figure 1 for showing that the countries' bliss points shift together, note first that the decrease in B^c needed to move the US economy downward on $B''B''$ must be equal absolutely to the increase in F^c needed to move it upward on FF; otherwise, the global money supply would change and affect the US price level. Then note that the decrease in B^c needed to move the US economy downward on $B'B'$ must be equal absolutely to the increase in F^c needed to move the EC economy up ward on $B'B'$. This is because the two economies are symmetrical, so that their BB and FF curves have the same properties; the triangles $ON''T''$ and $ON''T'$ are congruent, and $N''T''$ equals $N'T'$. By implication, the changes in B^c and F^c that define the shift in the US bliss point equal the changes that define the shift in the EC bliss point.

25 Under a floating exchange rate, it is better for EC fiscal policy to mimic US fiscal policy than to match a US deficit with an EC surplus. When both countries run identical budget deficits, the floating-rate outcomes come to look much like the pegged-rate outcomes (there is no change in the exchange rate), and decentralized monetary policies take the two economies to a common bliss point in the special pegged-rate case where $(1 - s\alpha)g = s$. It should be noted, however, that these fiscal-policy results do not always hold when the two economies are less than perfectly symmetrical; when they differ in the degree to which interest rates affect desired wealth and the demand for money, matching fiscal and monetary policies do not take them to a common bliss point under a pegged exchange rate. See Kenen, 'Coordination in an Asymmetric Model'.

26 Like the previous fiscal-policy result, however, this result may not go through when the economies are not completely symmetrical; see Kenen, 'Coordination in an Asymmetric Model'.

27 See, e.g., John Williamson, *The Exchange Rate System*, Policy Analyses in International Economics, 5, Revised Edition (Institute for International Economics, 1985), Williamson and Miller, *Targets and Indicators: A Blueprint for the International Coordination of Economic Policies*, Policy Analyses in International Economics, 22 (Institute of International Economics, 1987), and Peter B. Kenen, *Managing Exchange Rates* (Royal Institute for International Affairs and Routledge, 1988), ch. 2. See also Rudiger Dornbusch and Jeffrey Frankel, 'The Flexible Exchange Rate System: Experience and Alternatives', Working Paper 2464 (National Bureau of Economic Research, 1987), and Paul R. Krugman, *Exchange-rate Instability*, The Robbins Memorial Lectures (MIT Press, 1988), who make the argument cogently but do not endorse exchange-rate stabilization.

28 For references and comments, see Peter B. Kenen, 'Exchange Rate Management: What Role for Intervention?', *American Economic Review*, 77 (May 1987), pp. 194–9, and Kenen, *Managing Exchange Rates*, ch. 4.

29 There is still the need, however, to order the indicators more clearly; some of them relate to targets and others to instruments, and some of the instruments are targets as well. See Frankel, *Obstacles to International Macroeconomic Policy Coordination*, Princeton Studies in International Finance, 64 (International Finance Section, Princeton University, 1988), p. 2n, and Andrew Crockett and Morris Goldstein, *Strengthening the International Monetary System: Exchange Rates, Surveillance, and Objective Indicators*, Occasional Paper 50 (International Monetary Fund, 1987), ch. iii.

30 Sylvia Ostry, 'From Fine Tuning to Framework Setting in Macro-economic Management' in *Opportunities for the World Economy: OECD*

25th Anniversary Symposium (Organisation for Economic Cooperation and Development, 1986), pp. 9–10.

31   Gerald Holtham, 'International Policy Coordination: How Much Consensus is There?', *Brookings Discussion Papers in International Economics*, 50 (The Brookings Institution, September 1986), pp. 21–2.

32   Peter B. Kenen, 'What Role for IMF Surveillance?', *World Development*, 15 (1987), p. 1453. A similar but less ambitious formulation is proposed by Michael Artis and Sylvia Ostry, *International Economic Policy Coordination* (Royal Institute of International Affairs and Routledge & Kegan Paul, 1986), pp. 52–3 and 71. But they would use a single number, the growth rate of nominal GNP, as the basis for global and national targeting and for monitoring actual performance. It would be supplemented by use of the exchange rate, to check on the appropriateness of the policy mix adopted to achieve the principal target. When the exchange rate becomes a target in its own right, the formulation in the text and the Artis-Ostry framework begin to resemble the 'blueprint' in Williamson and Miller, *Targets and Indicators*, p. 2.

33   The lags might be shortened by using forecasts rather than the most recent actuals, but the relevant forecasts may not be accurate enough; see Peter B. Kenen and Stephen B. Schwartz, 'An Assessment of Macroeconomic Forecasts in the International Monetary Fund's World Economic Outlook', Working Paper G-86-04 (International Finance Section, Princeton University, December 1986). Frankel points out, however, that the revisions in actual data are sometimes as large as the errors in forecasts, so forecasts may not be more misleading than actuals (and have the virtue of shortening the lags); see Frankel, *Obstacles to Policy Coordination*, pp. 5–8. One result of the Kenen-Schwartz study should perhaps be noted here. The Fund's implicit forecasts for the growth rates of nominal GNP, the target variable mentioned in the previous note, proved to be more accurate than its forecasts for the growth rates of real GNP or for inflation rates.

34   Stanley Fischer, 'International Macroeconomic Policy Coordination' in M. Feldstein, ed., *International Economic Cooperation* (University of Chicago Press, 1988), p. 36.

Appendix

This appendix solves the two-country model outlined in the text and uses the solutions to prove key propositions concerning the behavior of the model. The solutions pertain to the short-run and long-run effects of five disturbances: a permanent shift in US or EC asset demand from the EC bond to the US bond (denoted by $dB_2^* > 0$); a permanent shift in US or EC consumer or government demand from the US good to the EC good (denoted by $dc_2^* > 0$); an open-market purchase of the domestic bond (denoted by $dB^c > 0$ or $dF^c > 0$); a balanced-budget increase in government spending (denoted by $dG_1 > 0$ or $dG_2' > 0$); and a temporary budget deficit that leaves in its wake a permanent increase in the supply of government debt (denoted by $gdB^* > 0$ or $gdF^* > 0$ in the short-run solutions and by $dB^* > 0$ or $dF^* > 0$ in the long-run solutions).

The short-run solutions

Results for the pegged-rate case are obtained by holding π at unity and allowing R to vary:

$$(1) \quad dR = \left(\frac{1}{A}\right) aW\phi[n(vdB^c - vdF^c) - (1-2a)(x_1 - x_2) + 2dc_2^*]$$

$$- \left(\frac{1}{A}\right) [s(1-2a)W\theta + n\delta Q]dB_2^*,$$

where

$$A = J_0 + aJ_t, J_0 = s(1-2a)J + aJ_t, J = W\theta + \alpha\delta Q, J_t$$
$$= nvW\phi + \delta Q, n = 2a + s\alpha(1-2a),$$
$$x_1 = s\alpha dG_1 + (1-s\alpha)gdB^*, x_2 = s\alpha dG_2' + (1-s\alpha)gdF^*,$$

(2) $dr_1 = -\left(\dfrac{1}{AJ}\right)[(aJ + \alpha J_0)vdB^c + a(nvW\phi\alpha - W\theta)vdF^c]$

$\qquad\quad - \left(\dfrac{1}{A}\right)[(nv)dB_2^* + dc_2^*]$

$\qquad\quad + \left(\dfrac{1}{AJ}\right)\left(\dfrac{1}{s}\right)[(J_0)x_1 + (aJ_t)x_2],$

(3) $dr_2 = -\left(\dfrac{1}{AJ}\right)[(aJ + \alpha J_0)vdF^c + a(nvW\phi\alpha - W\theta)vdB^c]$

$\qquad\quad + \left(\dfrac{1}{A}\right)[(nv)dB_2^* + dc_2^*]$

$\qquad\quad + \left(\dfrac{1}{AJ}\right)\left(\dfrac{1}{s}\right)[(aJ_t)x_1 + (J_0)x_2],$

(4) $dr_1 - dr_2 = \left(\dfrac{1}{A}\right)[n(vdF^c - vdB^c) + (1-2a)(x_1 - x_2)$

$\qquad\qquad\quad - (2nv)dB_2^* - 2dc_2^*],$

(5) $dQ_1 = \left(\dfrac{1}{AJ}\right)[A_1vdB^c + A_2vdF^c + v(A_1 - A_2)dB_2^*]$

$\qquad\quad - \left(\dfrac{1}{A}\right)(2avW\phi + \delta Q)dc_2^*$

$\qquad\quad + \left(\dfrac{1}{AJ}\right)\left(\dfrac{1}{s}\right)[\delta QJ_0 + s(1-2a)J(avW\phi)]x_1$

$\qquad\quad + \left(\dfrac{1}{AJ}\right)\left(\dfrac{1}{s}\right)a[\delta Q(2avW\phi + \delta Q) - s(1-2a)W\theta(vW\phi)]x_2,$

where

$$A_1 = W\theta(J_0), \ A_2 = W\theta(aJ_t), \ A_1 + A_2 = W\theta(A),$$
$$A_1 - A_2 = W\theta[s(1-2a)J],$$

(6) $dQ_2 = \left(\dfrac{1}{AJ}\right)[A_1 v dF^c + A_2 v dB^c - v(A_1 - A_2)dB_2^*]$

$\qquad + \left(\dfrac{1}{A}\right)(2av W\phi + \delta Q)dc_2^*$

$\qquad + \left(\dfrac{1}{AJ}\right)\left(\dfrac{1}{s}\right)[\delta Q J_0 + s(1-2a)J\,(av W\phi)]x_2$

$\qquad + \left(\dfrac{1}{AJ}\right)\left(\dfrac{1}{s}\right)a[\delta Q(2av W\phi + \delta Q) - s(1-2a)W\theta(v W\phi)]x_1.$

Terms such as A, J, etc., are positive unless otherwise indicated. The signs of the effects themselves are shown in the upper part of Table A-1. They are thoroughly symmetrical because the two economies are symmetrical.

Results for the floating-rate case are obtained by holding R at zero and allowing π to vary:

(7) $d\pi = \left(\dfrac{1}{AW}\right)\left(\dfrac{1}{A_\pi}\right)dR,$

where the dR are the changes in reserves given by equation (1), and

$$A_\pi = 2[(1-a)(U_0 + a\delta Q) + a\phi U_f], \ U_0 = s(1-2a)J + a\delta Q,$$
$$U_f = Q + s(1-2a)W,$$

(8) $dr_1 = -\left(\dfrac{1}{JA_\pi}\right)[2(1-a)(aJ + \alpha U_0) + a\alpha\phi U_f]v dB^c$

$\qquad + \left(\dfrac{1}{JA_\pi}\right)a[2(1-a)W\theta - \alpha\phi U_f]v dF^c - \left(\dfrac{1}{A_\pi}\right)U_f\left(\dfrac{1}{W}\right)dB_2^*$

$$+ \left(\frac{1}{JA_\pi}\right)\left(\frac{1}{s}\right)[2(1-a)U_0 + a\phi U_f]x_1$$

$$+ \left(\frac{1}{JA_\pi}\right)\left(\frac{1}{s}\right)a[2(1-a)\delta Q + \phi U_f]x_2 - \left(\frac{1}{A_\pi}\right)2(1-a)dc_2^*,$$

Table A-1 *Short-run effects of exogenous disturbances and policy changes*

Effect on	Open-market purchase by		Portfolio shift to	Fiscal expansion by		Demand shift to
	US	EC	US bond	US	EC	EC good
Pegged rate:						
Reserves[1]	+	−	−	−	+	+
US interest rate	−	?	−	+	+	−
EC interest rate	?	−	+	+	+	+
Difference[2]	−	+	−	+	−	−
US output	+	+	+	+	?	−
EC output	+	+	−	?	+	+
Floating rate:						
Exchange rate[1]	+	−	−	−	+	+
US interest rate	−	?*	−	+	+	−
EC interest rate	?*	−	+	+	+	+
Difference[2]	−	+	−	+	−	−
US output	+	?*	−	+	+	−
EC output	?*	+	+	+	+	+

1 Positive entries denote increases in EC reserves in the pegged-rate case and appreciations of the ecu (depreciations of the dollar) in the floating-rate case.
2 Change in US interest rate *less* change in EC interest rate.
* Negative when $U_2 > 0$.

$$(9) \quad dr_2 = -\left(\frac{1}{JA_\pi}\right)[2(1-a)(aJ + \alpha U_0) + a\alpha\phi U_f]vdF^c$$

$$+ \left(\frac{1}{JA_\pi}\right)a[2(1-a)W\theta - \alpha\phi U_f]vdB^c + \left(\frac{1}{A_\pi}\right)U_f\left(\frac{1}{W}\right)dB_2^*$$

$$+ \left(\frac{1}{JA_\pi}\right)\left(\frac{1}{s}\right)[2(1-a)U_0 + a\phi U_f]x_2$$

$$+ \left(\frac{1}{JA_\pi}\right)\left(\frac{1}{s}\right)a[2(1-a)\delta Q + \phi U_f]x_1$$

$$+ \left(\frac{1}{A_\pi}\right)2(1-a)dc_2^*,$$

$$(10) \quad dr_1 - dr_2 = \left(\frac{1}{A_\pi}\right)2(1-a)[n(vdF^c - vdB^c) + (1-2a)(x_1 - x_2)$$

$$- 2dc_2^*] - \left(\frac{1}{A_\pi}\right)2U_f\left(\frac{1}{W}\right)dB_2^*,$$

$$(11) \quad dQ_1 = \left(\frac{1}{JA_\pi}\right)[U_1 vdB^c - U_2 vdF^c - J(\delta Q)U_f\left(\frac{1}{W}\right)dB_2^*]$$

$$- \left(\frac{1}{A_\pi}\right)2\delta Q(1-a)dc_2^* + \left(\frac{1}{JA_\pi}\right)\left(\frac{1}{s}\right)\delta Q\{[2(1-a)U_0$$

$$+ a\phi U_f]x_1 + a[2(1-a)\delta Q + \phi U_f]x_2\},$$

where

$$U_1 = 2(1-a)(W\theta)U_0 + a(J + W\theta)\phi U_f,$$
$$U_2 = a\delta Q[\alpha\phi U_f - 2(1-a)W\theta] \gtrless 0,$$
$$U_1 - U_2 = (W\theta)A_\pi, \quad U_1 + U_2 = 2J[(1-a)s(1-2a)W\theta + a\phi U_f],$$

(12) $dQ_2 = \left(\dfrac{1}{JA_\pi}\right)[U_1 \, vdF^c - U_2 vdB^c - J(\delta Q)U_f\left(\dfrac{1}{W}\right)dB_2^*]$

$\qquad + \left(\dfrac{1}{A_\pi}\right)2\delta Q(1-a)dc_2^* + \left(\dfrac{1}{JA_\pi}\right)\left(\dfrac{1}{s}\right)\delta Q\{[2(1-a)U_0$

$\qquad + a\phi U_f]x_2 + a[2(1-a)\delta Q + \phi U_f]x_1\}.$

The signs of these effects are shown in the lower part of Table A-1.

The long-run solutions
These are the long-run solutions for the pegged-rate case:

(13) $dR^* = \left(\dfrac{1}{2N}\right)[N_t(vdB^c - vdF^c) + \alpha\delta Q(1-2a)(dG_1 - dG_2')$

$\qquad + \delta Q(dB^* - dF^*) - 2(\delta Q)dB_2^*] + \left(\dfrac{1}{2N}\right)[(1-2a)J$

$\qquad + 2aW\phi]\left(\dfrac{1}{a}\right)dc_2^*,$

where

$\qquad N = \quad vN_t + \delta Q, N_t = (1-2a)W\theta + 2aW\phi,$

(14) $dr_1^* = -\left(\dfrac{1}{2NJ}\right)(J + \alpha N)vdB^c - \left(\dfrac{1}{2NJ}\right)[(v\alpha - 1)W\theta$

$\qquad + \alpha 2 \, avW(\phi - \theta)]vdF^c + \left(\dfrac{1}{2NJ}\right)(vJ + N)dB^*$

$\qquad + \left(\dfrac{1}{2NJ}\right)[2avW(\phi - \theta) - (v\alpha - 1)\delta Q]dF^*$

$\qquad + \left(\dfrac{1}{2NJ}\right)\alpha[v(1-2a)J + N]dG_1$

$\qquad + \left(\dfrac{1}{2NJ}\right)\alpha(m\delta Q + 2avW\phi)dG_2'$

$$- \left(\frac{1}{2N}\right)[2vdB_2^* + m\left(\frac{1}{a}\right)dc_2^*],$$

where $v\alpha > 1$ but $m = [1 - v\alpha(1 - 2a)] \gtrless 0$,[1]

$$(15) \quad dr_2^* = -\left(\frac{1}{2NJ}\right)(J + \alpha N)vdF^c - \left(\frac{1}{2NJ}\right)[(v\alpha - 1)W\theta$$

$$+ \alpha 2avW(\phi - \theta)]vdB^c + \left(\frac{1}{2NJ}\right)(vJ + N)dF^*$$

$$+ \left(\frac{1}{2NJ}\right)[2avW(\phi - \theta) - (v\alpha - 1)\delta Q]dB^*$$

$$+ \left(\frac{1}{2NJ}\right)\alpha[v(1 - 2a)J + N]dG_2'$$

$$+ \left(\frac{1}{2NJ}\right)\alpha(m\delta Q + 2avW\phi)dG_1$$

$$+ \left(\frac{1}{2N}\right)[2vdB_2^* + m\left(\frac{1}{a}\right)dc_2^*],$$

$$(16) \quad dr_1^* - dr_2^* = \left(\frac{1}{N}\right)[(vdF^c - vdB^c) + v(dB^* - dF^*)$$

$$+ v\alpha(1 - 2a)(dG_1 - dG_2') - 2vdB_2^* - m\left(\frac{1}{a}\right)dc_2^*],$$

$$(17) \quad dp_1^* = \left(\frac{1}{2QJ}\right)[W\theta(vdB^c + vdF^c) + \delta Q(dB^* + dF^*)$$

$$+ \alpha\delta Q(dG_1 + dG_2')] - \left(\frac{1}{2Q}\right)(1 - 2a)\left(\frac{1}{a}\right)dc_2^*,$$

(18) $dp_2^* = \left(\dfrac{1}{2QJ}\right)[\ldots] + \left(\dfrac{1}{2Q}\right)\left(\dfrac{1}{a}\right)dc_2^*,$

(19) $dq_2^* = \left(\dfrac{1}{2QJ}\right)[\ldots] - \left(\dfrac{1}{2Q}\right)(1-2a)\left(\dfrac{1}{a}\right)dc_2^*,$

(20) $dq_2^* = dq_2'^* = \left(\dfrac{1}{2QJ}\right)[\ldots] + \left(\dfrac{1}{2Q}\right)(1-2a)\left(\dfrac{1}{a}\right)dc_2^*,$

where the terms [. . .] in equations (18), (19), and (20) are identical to the corresponding term in equation (17). The signs of these effects are shown in the upper part of Table A-2.

These are the long-run solutions for the floating-rate case:

(21) $d\pi^* = \left(\dfrac{2N}{QN_\pi}\right)dR^*,$

where the dR^* are the changes in reserves given by equation (13), and

$$N_\pi = (1 - 2a)J + 2N_0, \; N_0 = aW(\delta + \phi),$$

(22) $dr_1^* = \left(\dfrac{1}{JQN_\pi}\right)[aWJ + \alpha Q(1 - 2a)J + \alpha QN_0]vdB^c$

$\qquad - \left(\dfrac{1}{JQN_\pi}\right)aW(\alpha Q\phi - W\theta)vdF^c$

$\qquad + \left(\dfrac{1}{JN_\pi}\right)[(1 - a)J + N_0]dB^* + \left(\dfrac{1}{JN_\pi}\right)(N_0 - aJ)dF^*$

$\qquad + \left(\dfrac{1}{JN_\pi}\right)\alpha[(1 - 2a)J + N_0]dG_1 + \left(\dfrac{1}{JN_\pi}\right)\alpha(N_0)dG_2'$

$\qquad - \left(\dfrac{1}{QN_\pi}\right)[(Q)\,dB_2^* + (W)\,dc_2^*],$

$$(23) \quad dr_2^* = -\left(\frac{1}{JQN_\pi}\right)[aWJ + \alpha Q(1 - 2a)J + \alpha QN_0]vdF^c$$

$$-\left(\frac{1}{JQN_\pi}\right)aW(\alpha Q\phi - W\theta)vdB^c$$

$$+\left(\frac{1}{JN_\pi}\right)[(1 - a)J + N_0]dF^* + \left(\frac{1}{JN_\pi}\right)(N_0 - aJ)dB^*$$

$$+\left(\frac{1}{JN_\pi}\right)\alpha[(1 - 2a)J + N_0]dG_2' + \left(\frac{1}{JN_\pi}\right)\alpha(N_0)dG_1$$

$$+\left(\frac{1}{QN_\pi}\right)[(Q)\,dB_2^* + (W)\,dc_2^*],$$

$$(24) \quad dr_1^* - dr_2^* = \left(\frac{1}{QN_\pi}\right)[2aW + \alpha(1 - 2a)Q](vdF^c - vdB^c)$$

$$+\left(\frac{1}{N_\pi}\right)[(dB^* - dF^*) + \alpha(1 - 2a)(dG_1 - dG_2')]$$

$$-\left(\frac{1}{QN_\pi}\right)2[(Q)dB_2^* + (W)dc_2^*],$$

$$(25) \quad dp_1^* = \left(\frac{1}{JQN_\pi}\right)\{N_1vdB^c - N_2vdF^c + \delta Q[(1 - a)J + N_0]dB^*$$

$$+\delta Q(N_0 - aJ)dF^* + \alpha\delta Q[(1 - 2a)J + N_0]dG_1'$$

$$+\alpha\delta Q(N_0)dG_2' - \delta Q(J)dB_2^*\} - \left(\frac{1}{QN_\pi}\right)(\delta W)dc_2^*,$$

where

$$N_1 = W\theta[(1 - 2a)J + N_0] + (aW\phi)J, N_2 = aW\delta(\alpha Q\phi - W\theta)$$
$$\lessgtr 0, N_1 - N_2 = (W\theta)N_\pi, N_1 + N_2 = J(N_t),^2$$

$$(26) \quad dp_2^* = \left(\frac{1}{JQN_\pi}\right)\{\ldots\} + \left(\frac{1}{QN_\pi}\right)\left(\frac{1}{a}\right)[(1 - 2a)J + N_0 + aW\phi]dc_2^*,$$

(27) $dq_1^* = \left(\dfrac{1}{JQN_\pi}\right)\{\,\dots\,\} + \left(\dfrac{1}{QN_\pi}\right)[(1 - 2a)\,\alpha\delta G + N_t]dc_2^*,$

where the terms $\{\,\dots\,\}$ are identical to the corresponding terms in equation (25), and

(28) $dq_2'^* = \left(\dfrac{1}{JQN_\pi}\right)\{N_1vdF^c - N_2vdB^c + \delta Q[(1 - a)J + N_0]dF^*$

$+\quad \delta Q(N_0 - aJ)dB^* + \alpha\delta Q[(1 - 2a)J + N_0]dG_2'$

$+\quad \alpha\delta Q(N_0)dG_1 + \delta Q(J)dB_2^*\}$

$-\quad \left(\dfrac{1}{QN_\pi}\right)[(1 - 2a)\,\alpha\delta G + N_t]dc_2^*.$

The signs of these effects are shown in the lower part of Table A-2.

The own and cross effects of monetary policies

This section examines the properties of the BB and FF curves used in the text and of the reaction curves they are made to generate. It deals with outcomes for the US economy, but those for the EC are symmetrical.

Under a pegged exchange rate, equations (19) and (5) say that $dq_1^* = (W\theta/2QJ)vdB^c$ and $dQ_1 = (A_1/AJ)vdB^c$, where A, $A_1 > 0$. Therefore, the BB curve, showing the price and output effects of an open-market purchase by the US authorities, is positively sloped, and an open-market purchase ($dB^c > 0$) is represented by an upward movement along it. The same equations also say that $dq_1^* = (W\theta/2QJ)vdF^c$ and $dQ_1 = (A_2/AJ)vdF^c$, where $A_2 > 0$. Therefore, the FF curve, showing the effects of an open-market purchase by the EC authorities, is likewise positively sloped, and an open-market purchase is represented once again by an upward movement. Furthermore, the FF curve is steeper than the BB curve:

$(W\theta/2Q)(A/A_1) - (W\theta/2Q)(A/A_2) = (W\theta/2Q)\left(\dfrac{1}{A_1A_2}\right)(A_1 - A_2) > 0,$

Table A-2 *Long-run effects of exogenous disturbances and policy changes*

Effect on	Open-market purchase by US	Open-market purchase by EC	Portfolio shift to US bond	Higher spending by US	Higher spending by EC	Temporary tax cut by US	Temporary tax cut by EC	Demand shift to EC good
Pegged rate:								
Reserves[1]	+	−	−	+	−	+	−	+
US interest rate	−	?*	−	+	?	+	?	?
EC interest rate	?*	−	+	?	+	?	+	?
Difference[2]	−	+	−	+	−	+	−	?
Dollar prices:								
US output	+	+	0	+	+	+	+	−
EC output	+	+	0	+	+	+	+	+
Price indexes:								
US (in dollars)	+	+	0	+	+	+	?	−
EC (in ecu)	+	+	0	+	+	?	?	+
Floating rate:								
Exchange rate[1]	+	−	−	+	−	+	−	+
US interest rate	−	?*	−	+	+	+	?	−
EC interest rate	?*	−	+	+	+	?	+	+
Difference[2]	−	+	−	+	−	+	−	−
Dollar prices:								
US output	+	?*	−	+	+	+	?	−
EC output	+	?*	−	+	+	+	?	+
Price indexes:								
US (in dollars)	+	?*	−	+	+	+	?	+
EC (in ecu)	?*	+	+	+	+	?	+	−

See notes to Table A-1.

because $A_1 > A_2$. Note finally the outcomes in two special cases:

(1) When $dB^c = dF^c$, then $dq^*_1 = (W\theta/QJ)vdB^c$ and $dQ_1 = (W\theta/J)vdB^c$.

(2) When $dB^c = -dF^c$, then $dq^*_1 = 0$, and $dQ_1 = [(A_1 - A_2)/AJ]vdB^c > 0$.

Under a floating exchange rate, matters are more complicated. From equations (27) and (11), $dq^*_1 = (N_1/JQN_\pi)vdB^c$ and $dQ_1 = (U_1/JA_\pi)vdB^c$, where N_π, $A_\pi > 0$ and N_1, $U_1 > 0$, so the BB curve is positively sloped and an open-market purchase is represented by an upward movement. But the same equations say the $dq^*_1 = -(N_2/JQN_\pi)vdF^c$, and $dQ_1 = -(U_2/JA_\pi)vdF^c$, where $U_2 \gtrless 0$, so the FF curve can be positively or negatively sloped. Hereafter, however, I assume that $U_2 > 0$, so the FF curve will be positively sloped, but an open-market purchase by the EC authorities will be represented by a downward movement.[3]

Even under these conditions, however, the FF curve can be steeper or flatter than the BB curve. It is steeper when $(N_2/U_2) > (N_1/U_1)$. But $N_1 = (W\theta)N_\pi + N_2$ and $U_1 = (W\theta)A_\pi + U_2$, so the FF curve is steeper when $(N_2/N_\pi) > (U_2/A_\pi)$, which is in turn the condition under which the percentage change in q_1 induced by a change in F^c exceeds the corresponding change in Q_1. It holds when $nW\phi > [\alpha\phi U_f - 2(1 - a)W\theta]$, and both sides of this expression are positive when $U_2 > 0$.

Note finally the outcomes in the special cases considered earlier: (1) When $dB^c = dF^c$, then $dq^*_1 = [(N_1 - N_2)/JQN_\pi]vdB^c = (W\theta/JQ)vdB^c > 0$ and $dQ_1 = [(U_1 - U_2)/JA_\pi]vdB^c = (W\theta/J)vdB^c > 0$, which are the results obtained in the pegged-rate case.[4] (2) When $dB^c = -dF^c$, then $dq^*_1 = [N_1/QN_\pi]vdB^c > 0$ and $dQ_1 = 2[(1 - a)s(1 - 2a)W\theta + a\phi U_f](1/A_\pi)vdB^c > 0$.

Shifts in the policy-preference bliss points

The analysis in the text turns on the ways that various disturbances displace the countries' bliss points. This section proves some of the statements made there.

Under a pegged exchange rate, the US bliss-point shifts are obtained by setting $dQ_1 = dq^*_1 = 0$ and solving equations (5) and (19) for the requisite changes in B^c and F^c:

(29) $dB_1^c = \left(\dfrac{1}{v}\right)\left(\dfrac{1}{A_1 - A_2}\right)\left(\dfrac{J}{W\theta}\right)[(2QA_2)dq_1^s - (W\theta A)dQ_1^s]$,

(30) $dF_1^c = -\left(\dfrac{1}{v}\right)\left(\dfrac{1}{A_1 - A_2}\right)\left(\dfrac{J}{W\theta}\right)[(2QA_1)dq_1^s - (W\theta A)dQ_1^s]$,

where dq_1^s and dQ_1^s stand for the price and output effects of dB_2^*, dc_2^*, dG_1, dG_2', dB^*, and dF^*. The EC bliss-point shifts are obtained in the same way, using equations (6) and (20), and the two countries' bliss-point shifts can be compared by evaluating these expressions:

$$M^B = dB_1^c - dB_2^c = \left(\frac{1}{v}\right)\left(\frac{1}{A_1 - A_2}\right)\left(\frac{J}{W\theta}\right)[2Q(A_1 dq_2^s + A_2 dq_1^s),$$
$$- W\theta A\,(dQ_1^s + dQ_2^s)]\,,$$

$$M^F = dF_2^c - dF_1^c = \left(\frac{1}{v}\right)\left(\frac{1}{A_1 - A_2}\right)\left(\frac{J}{W\theta}\right)[2Q(A_1 dq_1^s + A_2 dq_2^s),$$
$$- W\theta A\,(dQ_1^s + dQ_2^s)]\,,$$

$$M_1 = dB_1^c + dF_1^c = -\left(\frac{1}{v}\right)\left(\frac{J}{W\theta}\right)2Q dq_1^s, \quad M_2 = dB_2^c + dF_2^c =$$
$$- \left(\frac{1}{v}\right)\left(\frac{J}{W\theta}\right)2Q dq_2^s.$$

When $M^B = M^F = 0$, the two countries' bliss points shift together. When $M_1 = M_2$, the new points lie on the same $-45°$ line (both governments would be perfectly content with the same amounts of monetary expansion or contraction in the world as a whole). To prove that the countries' bliss points shift differently, it is sufficient to show that $M_1 \neq M_2$ and thus to evaluate

$$M = M_1 - M_2 = \left(\frac{1}{v}\right)\left(\frac{J}{W\theta}\right)2Q(dq_2^s - dq_1^s).$$

The switch in demand for goods $(dc_2^* > 0)$ is the only exogenous shock for which $M \neq 0$, because $dq_1^s = -dq_2^s$. In all other instances, $dq_1^s = dq_2^s$ under a pegged exchange rate. But this does not prove that the bliss points shift together in those other instances. That happens if and only if $M^B = M^F = 0$.

With a switch in demand for bonds $(dB_2^* > 0)$, these last conditions hold, and the proof is trivial, because $dq_1^s = dq_2^s = 0$, and $dQ_1^s = -dQ_2^s$. With balanced-budget changes in government spending, they hold again, but the proof is more laborious. As $dq_1^s = dq_2^s = (1/2J)\alpha\delta(dG_1 + dG_2')$, we have $2Q(A_1 dq_2^s + A_2 dq_1^s) = (1/J)\alpha\delta Q(A_1 + A_2)(dG_1 + dG_2') = (1/J)\alpha\delta Q(W\theta A)(dG_1 + dG_2')$. But $WA\theta(dq_1^s + dq_2^s)$ has that same value, which completes the proof. The actual changes in the bliss-point coordinates are obtained from equations (29) and (30). For a balanced-budget increase in US spending,

$$dB_1^c = dB_2^c = -\left(\frac{1}{v}\right)\left(\frac{1}{W\theta}\right)\alpha(\delta Q + avW\phi)dG_1,$$

$$dF_1^c = dF_2^c = \left(\frac{1}{v}\right)\left(\frac{1}{W\theta}\right)\alpha(avW\phi)dG_1).$$

The effects of changes in B^* and F^* are harder to analyze, because the short-run output effects depend on the speed of adjustment, g, and the long-run price effects do not. It can indeed be shown that $M^B = M^F = 0$ for a particular value of g but not for any other. Note first that

$$M_1 = M_2 = -\left(\frac{1}{v}\right)\left(\frac{1}{W\theta}\right)\delta Q(dB^* + dF^*),$$

which says that both governments would be content with the same amount of monetary contraction. But

$$M^B = M^F = -\left(\frac{1}{v}\right)\left(\frac{A}{A_1 - A_2}\right)\delta Q[1 - \left(\frac{1}{s}\right)(1 - s\alpha)g](dB^* + dF^*),$$

which goes to zero if and only if $g = s/(1 - s\alpha)$. It should be noted, however, that offsetting fiscal-policy changes will stabilize outputs and prices when combined with appropriate monetary policies. When $dB^* = - dF^*$, $M^B = M^F = 0$, regardless of the value of g, and the bliss-point shifts will be the same. Suppose that the EC runs a budget deficit ($dF^* > 0$) that is offset exactly by a US budget surplus ($dB^* = - dF^* < 0$). From equations (29) and (30),

$$dB_1^c = dB_2^c = - dF_1^c = - dF_2^c$$
$$= \left(\frac{1}{v}\right)\left(\frac{1}{W\theta}\right)(\delta Q + 2avW\phi)\left(\frac{1}{s}\right)(1 - s\alpha)gdF^*.$$

There will be monetary expansion in the US (because Q_1 would fall without it) and an equal amount of monetary contraction in the EC (because Q_2 would rise without it). And because $dB^c + dF^c = dB^* + dF^* = 0$, there are no price changes in either country.

Under a floating exchange rate, the US bliss-point shifts are obtained from equations (11) and (27):

$$(31) \qquad dB_1^c = \left(\frac{1}{v}\right)\left(\frac{J}{H}\right)[Q(N_\pi U_2)dq_1^s - (A_\pi N_2)dQ_1^s],$$

$$(32) \qquad dF_1^c = \left(\frac{1}{v}\right)\left(\frac{J}{H}\right)[Q(N_\pi U_1)dq_1^s - (A_\pi N_1)dQ_1^s],$$

where $H = U_1 N_2 - U_2 N_1 \gtrless 0$.[5] The EC bliss points are obtained from equations (12) and (28), and the bliss-point shifts can be compared by evaluating

$$M_\pi^B = dB_1^c - dB_2^c = \left(\frac{1}{v}\right)\left(\frac{J}{H}\right)[QN_\pi(U_2 dq_1^s - U_1 dq_2^s)$$

$$- A_\pi(N_2 dQ_1^s - N_1 dQ_2^s)],$$

$$M_\pi^F = dF_2^c - dF_1^c = \left(\frac{1}{v}\right)\left(\frac{J}{H}\right)[QN_\pi(U_2 dq_2^s - U_1 dq_1^s)$$

$$- A_\pi(N_2 dQ_2^s - N_1 dQ_1^s)] \,,$$

$$M_{1\pi} = dB_1^c + dF_1^c = \left(\frac{1}{v}\right)\left(\frac{J}{H}\right)[QN_\pi(U_1 + U_2) dq_1^s$$

$$- A_\pi(N_1 + N_2) dQ_1^s],$$

$$M_{2\pi} = dB_2^c + dF_2^c = \left(\frac{1}{v}\right)\left(\frac{J}{H}\right)[QN_\pi(U_1 + U_2) dq_2^s$$

$$- A_\pi(N_1 + N_2) dQ_2^s],$$

$$M_\pi = M_{1\pi} - M_{2\pi} = \left(\frac{1}{v}\right)\left(\frac{J}{H}\right)[QN_\pi(U_1 + U_2)(dq_1^s - dq_2^s)$$

$$- A_\pi(N_1 + N_2)(dQ_1^s - dQ_2^s)],$$

which play the same roles as their pegged-rate counterparts.

With a switch in demand for goods ($dc_2^* > 0$), $dq_1^s = - dq_2^s > 0$ and $dQ_1^s = - dQ_2^s > 0$, so $M_\pi > 0$. The countries' bliss points shift differently. And this is what happens in all other instances.

With a switch in demand for bonds ($dB_2^* > 0$), $QN_\pi(dq_1^s - dq_2^s) = - 2\delta Q dB_2^*$ and $A_\pi(dQ_1^s - dQ_2^s) = - 2\delta Q U_f\left(\frac{1}{W}\right) dB_2^*$, so

$$M_\pi = - \left(\frac{1}{v}\right)\left(\frac{J}{H}\right) 2\delta Q \left(\frac{1}{W}\right)[W(U_1 + U_2) - (N_1 + N_2)U_f] dB_2^*$$

$$= \left(\frac{1}{v}\right)\left(\frac{J}{H}\right) 2\delta Q \left(\frac{J}{W}\right)(1 - 2a)W\theta(Q - sW) dB_2^*,$$

and $Q - sW = (1 - s\alpha)Q + s\alpha G > 0$, so $M_\pi > 0$.

With balanced-budget changes in government spending, $QN_\pi(dq_1^s - dq_2^s) = (1 - 2a)\alpha\delta Q(dG_1 - dG_2')$ and $A_\pi(dQ_1^s - dQ_2^s) = 2(1 - a)s (1 - 2a) \alpha\delta Q(dG_1 - dG_2')$, so

$$M_\pi = \left(\frac{1}{v}\right)\left(\frac{J}{H}\right)(1 - 2a)\alpha\delta Q[(U_1 + U_2) - 2(1 - a)s(N_1 + N_2)] \times$$

$$(dG_1 - dG_2') + \left(\frac{1}{v}\right)\left(\frac{J}{H}\right)(1 - 2a)\alpha\delta Q2J(a\phi)(Q - sW)(dG_1 - dG_2'),$$

and $Q - sW > 0$, as before, so $M_\pi > 0$.

With changes in B^* and F^*, the speed of adjustment becomes important, just as in the pegged-rate case, but there is no value of g for which $M_\pi = 0$. Here, $QN_\pi(dq_1^s - dq_2^s) = \delta Q(dB^* - dF^*)$ and $A_\pi(dQ_1^s - dQ_2^s) = 2(1 - a)\delta Q (1 - 2a) (1 - s\alpha)g(dB^* - dF^*)$, so

$$M_\pi = \left(\frac{1}{v}\right)\left(\frac{J}{H}\right)\delta Q[(U_1 + U_2) - 2(1 - a)(1 - 2a)(1 - s\alpha)g \times$$

$$(N_1 + N_2)](dB^* - dF^*) = \left(\frac{1}{v}\right)\left(\frac{J}{H}\right)\delta Q2J\{(1 - 2a)[(1 - a) \times$$

$$W\theta + aW\phi][s - (1 - 2a)(1 - s\alpha)g]$$

$$+ a\phi[Q - W(1 - 2a) (1 - s\alpha)g]\}(dB^* - dF^*).$$

When $g = s/[(1 - s\alpha)(1 - 2a)]$, one term vanishes, but the other becomes $a\phi(Q - sW)$, which appeared in previous cases. There is indeed no simple case in which $M_\pi = 0$. Furthermore, fiscal and monetary policies cannot be combined to stabilize outputs and prices, which was possible in the pegged-rate case. As $M_\pi = 0$ when $dB^* = dF^*$, one country must match the other country's policy rather than offset it. When this is done, moreover, $M_\pi^B = M_\pi^F = 0$ if and only if $g = s/(1 - s\alpha)$, which was the result obtained in the pegged-rate case.[6]

Devaluation to neutralise a switch in demand for goods.

A switch in demand for goods ($dc_2^* > 0$) produces a difference in bliss-point shifts whether the exchange rate is pegged or floating. But a once-for-all change in a pegged rate (a devaluation of the dollar) can deal with this problem. The short-run and long-run effects of an exchange-rate change are obtained from the pegged-rate version of the model by adding the exchange-rate change to the list of disturbances. The output and price effects are written here as addenda to equations (5), (6), (19), and (20), along with the effects of the switch in demand for goods:

(5a) $dQ_1 = \left(\dfrac{1}{A}\right)[aA^\pi d\bar{\pi} - (2avW\phi + \delta Q)dc_2^*],$

where

$A^\pi = (2avW\phi + \delta Q)U_f + 2(1 - a)Wv(W\theta)s(1 - 2a),$

(6a) $dQ_2 = -\left(\dfrac{1}{A}\right)[aA^\pi d\bar{\pi} - (2avW\phi + \delta Q)dc_2^*],$

(19a) $dq_1^* = \left(\dfrac{1}{2Q}\right)[Qd\bar{\pi} - (1 - 2a)\left(\dfrac{1}{a}\right)dc_2^*],$

(20a) $dq_2'^* = -\left(\dfrac{1}{2Q}\right)[Qd\bar{\pi} - (1 - 2a)\left(\dfrac{1}{a}\right)dc_2^*].$

Therefore, $dq_1^* = dq_2'^* = 0$ when $d\bar{\pi} = \left(\dfrac{1}{Q}\right)(1 - 2a)\left(\dfrac{1}{a}\right)dc_2^*.$

Substituting this exchange-rate change into equations (5a) and (6a),

$dQ_1 = - dQ_2 = \left(\dfrac{1}{A}\right)[A_\pi \left(\dfrac{1}{Q}\right)(1 - 2a) - (2avW\phi + \delta Q)]dc_2^*].$

But this means that $dq_1^s = dq_2^s = 0$ and $dQ_1^s + dQ_2^s = 0$, so $M^B = M^F = 0$. The two countries' bliss points shift together after the exchange rate is changed to offset the long-run price effects of the exogenous switch in demand.

Notes

I am grateful to John Leahy for checking and correcting this Appendix.

[1] As $v = (Q/L)$ and $\alpha = (W/Y^d)$ initially, $v\alpha = (Q/Y^d)(W/L)$; but $Q > Y^d$ and $W > L$. Nevertheless, $m = -(1/Y^d)[G + (Q/L)(B_1 - B_2)] \gtrless 0$ because $B_1 \gtrless B_2$. Under the assumptions made above, each country's holdings of the other country's bond are smaller initially than its total holdings of domestic assets, so that $B_1 + L_1 > \pi F_1$. But $\pi F_1 = aW = B_2$, so $B_1 - B_2 > -L_1$. The stricter condition $B_1 - B_2 > 0$ could have been obtained by assuming that each country's holdings of the other's bond was smaller than its holdings of the domestic bond.

[2] Rewrite N_2 as $aW\delta[\alpha Q(\phi - \theta) + (\alpha Q - W\theta)]$, so $N_2 > 0$ when $\phi > \theta$, as assumed in the text, because $\alpha Q - W = \alpha Q - \alpha(Q - G) = \alpha G$.

[3] As $U_2 = aQ\delta[\alpha\phi U_f - 2(1 - a)W\theta] = aQ\delta(\alpha U_f)(\phi - \theta) + aQ\delta[\alpha U_f - 2(1 - a)W]\theta$, it follows that $U_2 > 0$ when $\phi > \theta$ and $\alpha U_f > 2(1 - a)W$. The second condition is satisfied when

$$(G/Q) > (1 - s\alpha)(1 - 2a)/[1 + (1 - s\alpha)(1 - 2a)]$$

and thus sets a lower bound on the size of the public sector.

[4] That is because $dR = dR^* = d\pi = d\pi^* = 0$ when $dB^c = dF^c$, and there is no observable difference between the pegged-rate and floating-rate outcomes.

[5] Clearly, $H > 0$ when FF is steeper than BB, and $H < 0$ when the relationship is reversed.

[6] When $dB^* = dF^*$, then $dR = dR^* = d\pi = d\pi^* = 0$, so pegged-rate and floating-rate cases are the same. Therefore, identical changes in B^* and F^* will lead to identical bliss-point shifts if and only if they would do so under a pegged exchange rate.